Mark My Words

Mark My Words

LETTERS OF A BUSINESSMAN TO HIS SON

G. Kingsley Ward

PRENTICE HALL PRESS

New York

Published by Prentice Hall Press
A Division of Simon & Schuster, Inc.
Gulf + Western Building
One Gulf + Western Plaza
New York, NY   10023

PRENTICE HALL PRESS is a trademark of Simon & Schuster, Inc.

This is a revised edition of a book first
published by McCrary Publishing Inc. in 1985.

Library of Congress Cataloging-in-Publication Data

Ward, G. Kingsley.
Mark my words.
Previously published as: Letters of a businessman to his son.
1. Success in business.   I. Title.
HF5386.W23   1986   650.1   85-30047
ISBN 0-13-531518-2

Manufactured in the United States of America
10 9 8 7 6 5 4 3 2 1

First Prentice Hall Press Edition

This book is dedicated to
KING and JULIE

to all young people interested in business

and to their future

Be not afraid of greatness:
some are born great,
some achieve greatness,
and some have greatness
thrust upon them.
— WM. SHAKESPEARE
Twelfth Night

ACKNOWLEDGMENT

Editing is a difficult, time-consuming task—far more difficult and nerve-racking if it is attempted on behalf of a businessman-cum-writer husband trying to express some of his thoughts in written form. I know, because my wife, Adele, took on the next-to-impossible project of the first edit—trying to retain what I had to say, *my* way, with all the commas and periods in their proper places and all the i's dotted and the t's crossed. Her marriage vows of 1959, "for better or for worse," had not included this form of drudgery, but we are both happy to say that now that it is all over, our marriage is still intact and our household has resumed normality. On the positive side, I think Adele enjoyed this shared effort. I did. And I believe the end result made for an even stronger partnership between us. As an artist, she had the patience to complete the task.

And I am grateful.

CONTENTS

CONTENTS

PREFACE

Having survived two serious operations within four years, I quickly learned that none of us goes on forever, and it appeared a provident move to me to look at estate plans for my family. In so doing, I decided my businesses should continue under family ownership. Because my son was only fifteen and my daughter only seventeen at the time, and in case I were not around to assist them in person when they were older, an important part of my estate planning became my desire to impart to them some of the lessons I had learned the hard way in the corporate world that might make the road a little less bumpy for them. Toward this end, I started setting a few words down on paper.

Our schools and universities teach the minutest details on the widest range of subjects, but almost no assistance is given on many of the topics I believe are of paramount value to any students contemplating business careers. As I began writing, it became increasingly clear to me that a terrible amount of learned information passes away in the night wasted with each soul who leaves this earth. There were and are many others better equipped than I to write about some of the pitfalls of the business world. Alas, few have chosen to do so.

In my view, *common sense* is probably the best weapon with which to enter the battles of the business world. Regretfully, common sense seems to elude many people during their combats—as so often does its brother, *responsibility.* Yet these characteristics are the very basics of success.

I cannot remember when I first showed any promise for the business field, but I can well remember trying to hurdle the many pitfalls that confronted me—the same struggles that still confront every young person attempting to establish himself in this world. Some of the pitfalls seemed more like falling off the side of a huge mountain at the time, but fortunately I was able to climb my way back up to start over—though often only to a rung of the ladder a good deal lower than the one on which I had lost my footing. Thomas Henry Huxley said, "There is the greatest practical benefit in making a few failures early in life." A few failures, fine—but the trick is to survive those few and not become addicted to failure as some do, largely because of a lack of direction and a will or desire to learn the ground rules of getting ahead.

These words are written with the hope that they will help eliminate some of the potholes of life—or at least provide the means of skirting, going around, or jumping over them. To young people entering the business world —and to some already immersed in it—I would like to stress that learning does not stop the day you leave the classroom. In fact, your real lessons are only then beginning, and they will require more emphasis, energy, and study than ever before if success is to knock at your door. (By the way, I would suggest you bang on its door first, not wait around for *it* to come knocking at yours.)

There are numerous quotations contained herein—words of many philosophers, poets, writers, leaders, and statesmen whose thoughts have been recorded down through the centuries for posterity. They are in abundance for a simple reason: most agonies or joys of life or *common sense* have been contemplated by far greater minds than mine, and in many cases, many of my thoughts or points of view have already been penned and expressed far more succinctly than my mental capacities or writing skills permit. I have therefore borrowed freely from some great minds to strengthen, underscore, or clarify much of what I have to say.

Somewhere along the way in life each of us hears that the brain is capable of producing a great deal more than most of us ask of it. Charles Dudley Warner put it this way: "What small potatoes we all are, compared with what we might be!" I subscribe to Mr. Warner's theory wholeheartedly—and grieve over the wastage wrought through neglect, which we bring upon ourselves by not learning how to expand our brain power.

It goes without saying that hard work is essential for achieving success. However, more important is how one *channels* his work efforts toward success. I have seen many people work extremely long, arduous hours with very limited success. Why? Usually because they have been unable to apply common sense to the harnessing of an effective directional plan and organized methods of application.

Attaining success requires the setting of *goals* in one's life. Set those down for yourself and then carefully map the routes that will lead directly toward them. Plan your career along a realistic path. Perhaps not for you the desire of a presidency—but surely, are we not all capable of doing a lot more with our lifetimes than what society seems to demand, request, or require? I heartily believe so.

This book has been written in the masculine gender; father to son. However, my words are offered to anyone interested in business—with the sincerest hope that they will be found useful. It was written singularly to my son because at the time of writing, my daughter's interests and intentions for her future were focused outside the business world. Since she has now changed her mind and her course in life, and if I were beginning these letters now, they would be addressed with equal love and enthusiasm to both my daughter and my son.

It is to my great delight that my daughter recently decided to enter the world of business. In today's Western society we are continually moving ahead in our quest for knowledge and its application to every facet of our existence. I am delighted that in the course of our search, the realization has begun to dawn that women not only comprise 50 percent of the world's populace, but 50 percent of the world's human capabilities and aspirations.

Increasingly, women are participating in business at executive levels and contributing vital perspectives that regretfully—to the detriment of society—have been disregarded or ignored in the past. So it is with great enthusiasm that my wife and I observe our daughter's desire and choice to enter the business field, and we will observe her and our son's progress with great interest, pride, and delight.

Dare to dream—dare to try—dare to fail—dare to succeed.

THE LETTERS

Challenge

$\mathcal{D}$ear Son:

I understand you have just received a letter stating you have been accepted for enrollment at St. Andrew's this fall. It is with some surprise that I learn you are less than eager to join this outstanding and excellent school.

I daresay many other young fellows would jump at the chance of joining this elite college, and it is unfortunate the great majority never will belong to it, because of the substantial cost involved, geographical restrictions, or inadequate scholastic achievements. Fortunately, none of these pertain to you—and with so much going for you, your negativeness about this opportunity leaves me somewhat shaken and perplexed and more than a little concerned.

It is not a father's place to push his son in directions for which the boy has no heart; more sons have had their lives interfered with this way than I care to think about. All I wish to point out to you is this: we all go around this world only once—so make the most of it!

Many are the people I know who at the age of thirty-five, forty-five, fifty-five, say to me, "I really missed out in life." About 90 percent of them have excuses, rational-

3

izing why life passed them by, why they never accomplished anything; the other 10 percent honestly admit they just did not accept the *challenges* life placed in front of them during their earlier years. I feel sorry for these people because in many cases they probably had everything going for them when that gauntlet was tossed their way—except the courage to pick it up.

Facing new opportunities that involve a change of lifestyle, living patterns, usage of time, is something many people fail to rise up to and accept. The hardest thing I ever did was to leave my home in a small town and go a thousand miles to a big city where there was not one person I knew. But that was the only path to success for me, and as much as I hated it—for it was a terribly lonely path—there was always that *goal* ahead: the goal I had set *by* myself, *for* myself, and I insisted on at least trying for it. Accepting that challenge changed my whole life.

The challenge you are facing now—tackling this new school—is a crossroad in your life, and if you cannot even try *testing* your footing on this new, statistically proven surer road to success because it might be too demanding, then you have already—at a very young age —started the pattern that twenty or thirty years from now will lead you to say "life passed me by."

> There is a tide in the affairs of men,
> Which, taken at the flood, leads on to fortune;
> Omitted, all the voyage of their life
> Is bound in shallows and in miseries.
> —WM. SHAKESPEARE
> *Julius Caesar*

Let us examine this challenge. If you decide to try it, how much harm can it do to you? No one is going to cut off your arm, put you in jail, or take away your motorcycle if you do not succeed. On the contrary, if you do get your ass beat off, then welcome to the club, because I have that happen to me in the business world very frequently—to the point now that I never give a failure a second thought. Yesterday is for dreamers. I am too busy thinking about *today's* battles.

Failure is both a funny and a sad thing. We worry so much about it coming our way that we cultivate ulcers, nervous breakdowns, tics, rashes, or hot flashes. Yet on the odd occasion when that dark day of doom does come around, we find it isn't really quite as bad as we thought it would be; for some reason, the way our minds sometimes tend to work overtime building up possible disasters is very often very far off the mark.

According to your evaluation of this new school, all the students are expected to pull off straight A's and do; they are all 6′4″ tall; they are all 250-pound athletes—and to boot, they all execute dynamic projects in record time and enviable fashion.

Let me tell you—no, let me quietly explain to you: the percentage of outstanding students at this school is no higher than that at your present school; the only difference is this group *tries* harder, therefore it achieves more. You, as most of us mortals in this world do, fall into a middle or average category with respect to brains, abilities, or what have you—and that is not the worst place to be, believe me. However, when you join a school or group of this caliber, your work patterns and efforts automatically move up in such a way that you hardly notice because *you are going along with the tide*—one that is *not* going out.

I know you don't know the meaning of the term *process of osmosis*, so I will define it for you: in simple terms, it means that if one becomes totally immersed in any particular facet of life, one cannot help but absorb that facet. Immersion among a group of higher caliber students will result in a higher rate of success for you because knowing you, you are not the type to sit back and let the world pass you by. Instead, you seem to want to get out and keep ahead of it. At least that has been my impression of you to date.

Challenge is treated differently by different people. Some people are so afraid of life they accomplish about as much as a cow in pasture does; others thrive on challenges and are constantly looking for new ones. Between the two extremes is the denominator called *common sense,* which should separate the challenges that lead nowhere from those that lead somewhere. After a while you learn that challenge is a part of life—and you learn how to take it in your stride knowing that you will win most of the time, lose some of the time, but become a better man either way for having tried.

As Gabriel Biel said in 1495, "No one conquers who does not fight."

But whichever way you accept this or *any* challenge of your life, I will remain always,

Most faithfully,

Your Loving Father

Education

$\mathcal{D}$ear Son:

Most people think of education as having only to do with school. Well, that is a good place to *start.* In your case, your high school has a particularly good record for turning out fine students, and I expect one reason for its success as such an excellent institution is the emphasis it places on discipline. Of course, lots of good men and women make it without ever having attended this type of school—but the main reason is still the same: discipline. In this case, mostly *self-*discipline. That is the key ingredient that separates those who make it from those who do not. But a good school and a good mixture of people to enjoy it with is certainly an advantageous start. Combine these somewhat uncontrollable external forces with some good internal characteristics and it becomes pretty hard to keep a determined fellow down.

Within the framework of your formal schooling it is important for you to bring an element of inquisitiveness to the classroom. A *desire* to learn makes the act of studying and learning a delight. Too many of your fellow students are too busy complaining about the teachers and *the system* to tend to their studies, which, after all, are the primary reason for being in school. The system has not changed in the thirty years since I was at college and it probably won't alter much over the next thirty years (along with most of the educators). So instead of complaining about it, why not just get on with *beating* "the system"!

I applaud your desire to enter the business world. To a young fellow, it looks quite rosy: big car, travel, meals in the best restaurants. I envisage your love of a dollar riding high. Well, it *is* a good life *if*—and it is a *big* "if" —you find your particular niche in it, for the business world is very large and very complex. It is also a world full of bankruptcies and of people who die early due to its stress. To be as prepared as possible for avoiding some of these and the many other pitfalls that business presents daily, map out your next ten years of training *now*.

In the selection of your courses, do not be too eager to pick only those that solely relate to business. A person with a little worldly knowledge is as valuable as he is rare. There are countless subjects to choose from that will give you a wider perspective of this world and make you a better businessman one day—Political Science, History, Geology, Astronomy—to mention but a few.

According to the English writer John Dryden, everything in the world is good for something, and I believe that wholeheartedly. I would recommend you take one new subject every year that will give you a wider perspective, a new or different outlook on life. You never know what field of industry you might eventually become involved in or how valuable even a *little* knowledge might be once you're winding your way through those mine fields of the business world.

8

University education is designed to expand your brains, train you to work hard, teach you how to organize your hours and days, meet many people, play sports, chase girls, drink beer, and enjoy life. (Just don't place *too* much emphasis on the last three "subjects" since these somehow seem to get ample share of one's days [and nights] with very little expenditure of hard work or effort.)

Also attainable at university is Francis Bacon's formula for success. He writes, "Reading maketh a full man; conference, a ready man; and writing, an exact man." Now *there's* a combination of talents; a surefire trio for anyone aiming for the top! The day you can leave university feeling you are well read, you know you can write, and you have a knowledge of people—you are ready to enter the real world. This is the formula I have personally tried to follow and build on. And I hasten to add that at *no* stage have I ever found there was not a lot more to learn. One does grow old ever learning.

At your age of eighteen, it is imperative to have a *vision* in front of you of what you want to be doing in ten years' time. That period between twenty and thirty years of age is the most crucial of all learning periods. If you do not get the required study you need for your future work accomplished during these years, you will more than likely not get it done at all. By age thirty, your life becomes one of wife and children, a mortgage, a job— with precious little time left over for studying for a career. Some even say that at this age the brain does not absorb information as efficiently as it does in earlier years.

Your aim or goal in life for age thirty might be termed only a dream or a fantasy right now; nevertheless it must still be kept at the forefront of your mind as your *incentive* or *motivation* at this point. Without some goal or other to shoot for, it is almost impossible to keep up long hours of study. Your goal must be kept in front of you each new day you put your feet on the floor, for only this will get you through all the rough spots—the arduous work, a failed exam, a poor mark on an essay, a boring professor, or a difficult but compulsory course.

Once you have determined your goal, doggedly pursue finding out as much about it as you possibly can. Many people say, "I think I'll be a lawyer," without the foggiest idea what a lawyer does all day, without an inkling of the many facets of law in which he or she might end up involved. Makes far more sense to first talk to someone in the profession—but to someone with a balanced outlook on life; no use talking to a person so caught up in his chosen field that he considers law the one and only topic in the world nor, on the other hand, to one who hates his chosen work. A good "counselor" will recommend a course of study you should pursue and, more importantly, he will tell you what to expect when you get to the finishing line and start practicing law yourself.

Neglecting such preliminaries can easily not only result in the loss of valuable time, but, quite conceivably, in a lifetime of feeling entrapped in a profession not as palatable as you might have wished versus one you *could* have had if you had taken the time and trouble to select it more carefully in the first place.

Once you have completed your review and chosen what you want to be—lawyer, certified public accountant, marketing executive, whatever—try to get some work in your chosen field during summer recess. While you have no recourse but to be very deeply immersed in your books during this period of your life, at the same time do not lose sight of this fact: it will still be the *practical execution* of your future work that will determine the measure of your success within your chosen profession. So pull whatever strings that you, your old man, your uncle, great-uncle, or any friend can arrange for you to help you find summer employment in the same field as your intended future endeavor. Thomas Huxley said, "The great end of life is not knowledge but action." I would add this addendum: "—action as dictated by the *use* of your knowledge."

During my summers, I worked in the accounting offices of the local paper mill. It was excellent experience. However, I would like you to especially note the following episode during this period of my life. One summer I could not get the job in accounting and I ended up working in one of the physically toughest, dirtiest jobs in the mill: eight hours a day, six days a week, on shift work. That left me with two major impressions: the work some men had to spend their whole working lifetimes performing, and the tough working conditions under which they were spending such a great portion of their lifetimes. I made certain I would not have to be one of them again. Do not *waste* that time you get away from your books. Plan ahead and use it getting some on-the-job experience in your chosen field. At your stage in life, most everything is a new experience. Better to learn it sooner than later.

While you sit around quaffing a beer or two with your friends, I know the conversation at times turns to talk of taking a year off from school to *see the world*. Coincidentally, these times usually occur just when studying has gotten a little tougher or heavier, or just before a poor set of marks is about to land on the old man's desk and hit the fan. There are no newer or more valid grounds for talk of such hiatuses since my college days, I am sure; probably just as large a percentage of students now as then convince themselves for the same reasons how educational it is to travel around the world with a pack on one's back and no money.

On some days it sure does look good. But my personal opinion is that most of the students contemplating such excursions are just too lazy to study any more and needing a way out, they yield to the belief they could only benefit from such an educational jaunt, so off they go to see the world. The saddest thing is, statistics prove only a rare bird ever returns to his hallowed halls of learning.

If you feel you need a backpack trip around Europe, I suggest you use the time you have off from school between May 1st and September 1st: ample time for getting this kind of education. And if you are *seriously* entertaining thoughts in your head of this nature, I will offer you a deal: take the year off and travel without any funds—or go in May at *my* expense. You might call this bribery. I do, but I offer it unabashedly because I know how difficult it is—once that brain has been given too long a holiday—to get it back in gear again for studying four to five hours a day. Plus, I hate to see a house left half built.

Assuming your career in university comes to a successful conclusion, per the advice of the senior people in your chosen profession (the best advice you could find), your next five to six years must be devoted to further study and experience. As a prejudiced certified public accountant, I obviously consider my profession a very fine training ground for anyone preparing to enter the business world. A Master of Business Administration and several years in a marketing position is a good alternative.

With the help of a good tutor during these years and lots of hard work on your part, you should be able to progress rapidly and advance right to the top. A poor teacher might sidetrack you and cause you to hit some detours along the way. Should this occur, you would more than likely require a few extra years for getting the hang of it. But either way, remember, if there is a lack of *hard work* on your part, you will need to update your résumé and send out some applications for a new job. Just don't bother sending one to *me*; I hate sending out rejection notices. Closer to about age thirty, if you are still interested in running the family businesses, I will gladly accept your job application.

Should you join our companies at about this stage, you will have another five to ten years of learning—and more learning—before you become an experienced executive. However, there will be no exams to get boned up on, no report cards—only monthly profit-and-loss statements informing you whether you are passing or failing in the real world. It will take you at least five years to get to know the businesses we are in—our customers, suppliers, employees, management staff, the coordinating of external forces (those you cannot do much about), and the coordinating of internal forces (those you can do something about). Now you might be ready to enjoy that big car, travel, and those expensive restaurants.

Business is like a fragile vase—beautiful in one piece,

but once broken, damn hard to put back together again to its original form. So, in the words of Sam Butler:

And look before you ere you leap;
For as you sow, ye are like to reap!

Respectfully,

Teacher

On Success

$\mathcal{D}$ear Son:

Recently I heard a teacher expounding on the trials and pitfalls facing the sons of successful fathers; the tribulations of growing up in the big wakes of high achievers. He stated it was one of a young man's most difficult adjustments because the young man never feels he can be as good as his father. Apparently many boys do not even try. They give up before even *starting* to tap their own abilities and resources. Sad to hear.

It occurred to me that you too might be harboring some notions of this nature and just in case you are, before they take hold of your mind as an excuse for backing off in life, let me tell you a few things that happened to me along the way.

In high school I had an average of 60 in the ninth grade, 65 in the tenth grade, 75 in the eleventh grade. I then transferred to university, but as you can see for yourself, it was not because I was any brain; that was just the particular school system in my area. I got through my first two years of university, but with standings that were nothing to shout about despite a lot of studying. And

15

work I did, I assure you, because nothing came into my noggin easily.

Then I failed the first exams of my certified public accountant's course. I could not believe it! I was crushed. Here I was with six years of university—*finished! Through!* Needless to say, I breathed one great sigh of relief when I was allowed to rewrite my exams the following year.

Having assessed why I had failed the first time, I made certain it would not happen again. It didn't. It had been no big mystery to figure out: I simply had not worked hard enough. I have ever since.

The work or study habit is hard to come by. It requires a natural desire to learn, it requires practicing the art of concentration, but most of all, it requires a spirit for hard work. All these positive, productive attitudes can easily be accomplished by 90 percent of the populace. Few accomplish them.

If you think all my endeavors have always been successful, then you are unaware of details concerning a large part of my life. Successful people appear to be traveling along one continual, successful road. What is not apparent is the perseverance it takes following each defeat to keep you on that road. No one I know of has ever experienced one success after another without defeats, failures, disappointments, and frustrations galore along the way. Learning to overcome those times of agony is what separates the winners from the losers. How many times have I talked about the people who are so afraid of failure they never even enter the race?

Every failure teaches one something—and some failures teach more than others. Failing my first set of cpa exams has remained with me for the past twenty-five years. The lesson learned? You had better work hard, for you are not going to make it otherwise. With any maxi-

*D*ear Son:

mum effort, most things fall into place. But the race is not necessarily won by the swiftest; it is won by people who *learn* from past races and put those lessons to good use.

Remember, people tend to look upon successful people as they appear to be *now*. They overlook the many years of hard work, failure, frustrations, and problems—all encountered, lots conquered—all along the way.

With an objective in sight, one constantly tries attaining a higher level of achievement. So those objectives you set for yourself are vitally important.

Now the next time you feel inclined to look at dad and think his boots are too big for your feet to ever fill, remember, too, that you have a big head start on the old man. Your advantages? Your school work for one, with, to date, a much higher academic achievement level than I had. Your exposure to life; at your age, I had hardly ever left my small town and knew nothing about the big city and its complexities. Your parents; mom and I can steer you toward a few good doors into life. My mother and dad were sixty-five when I was your age and as dear, loving, and wonderful as they were, they knew nothing of the business and social environments in which we exist.

At high school you achieved the honor of being selected one of the officers of your school. You were captain of the second basketball team. Despite three knee operations, you played football for three years. Your leadership qualities are all there—all in clear view.

Consider. You have already accomplished far more than I had at your stage. Why should the future be any different?

Morals, spirit, hard work, and responsibility are choices you must make daily. How you decide to conduct yourself in society tests your moral fiber; how you perform on the football field or basketball court exemplifies what type of spirit you possess; the amount and quality of time and concentration you devote to your studies establishes diligence or lack thereof. To all of this, bring your mind to bear on each act you perform in daily living and ask yourself, "Is this being responsible?" For in the end, how *responsible* you are determines how *successful* you are.

Your achievements to date are many—already the accoutrements of a successful young man decidedly on his way up. Think about it. You have only to finish what you have already so well started, only to continue the successes waiting to be continued.

The old man? Unbeatable? Hell, eventually you'll run circles round him!

Sincerely,

Your No.1 Cheerleader

Stopping the Momentum

$\mathcal{D}$ear Son:

Your mid term report just arrived and it has some peculiar looking letters on it such as D, D–, and C–. I had not seen these before, so I asked a friend of mine what they meant. From the reply I got, I rather suspect that big smile of self-satisfaction that almost blinded us all following your first-year results has kind of dimmed. However, I assume there were sufficient smiles and adequate joviality during your first term to carry you over for a while. I hope. Or did you waste too much of all that spare time you had in sleeping?

You have probably noticed that pushing a car uphill is hard work. While you can stop for a rest, you must *finish* the job or chances are your car will slide all the way back to the bottom of the hill. Then you have to start pushing all over again. Work is like that. So is studying. No matter how much you did yesterday, unless you keep chipping away at it, you lose *momentum*. Once your momentum is gone, erosion of all your past efforts starts setting in because you are off the track that finishes the job. In your case, your job is getting through university.

Although it is a few years back, I do remember some

very bright boys in my first-year classes. How I envied them! Their high marks seemed to come so easily, while I had to work like hell for my crummy B–'s. But second year turned out to be another story. For one thing, I learned that some of those bright boys were *coasting* on the momentum they had built up in high school, where they had worked hard. Still, at the end of this year, it was an enormous amazement to me to learn that our class had lost about 35 percent of its people. Some had flunked, some had just plain quit, some had changed courses to easier ones. And a lot of them were the bright fellows I had started out with! They had just run out of their tremendous high-school momentum.

You see, because they had had an easy, lazy first year, they figured second year would be the same: an easy piece of cake. By the time some of them realized what had happened, it was too late. They were no longer able to discipline their minds enough to handle the required concentration that would put them back on their work tracks. In other words, they could not reverse the *downward* momentum.

After you have lived a few more years, you will observe that life is an uphill battle; as soon as one project is accomplished, another looms up. If you are not in stride, ready to take on new efforts, your failure rate in life will be high. That is what separates successful men from those who never make it.

At this juncture, I perceive no evidence of your having coasted during your first year. However, what I *do* perceive is that you have forgotten that life at certain stages is like paddling our canoe up the rivers we have covered. Stop paddling when you are heading upstream and, man, that current sure soon takes you downriver in a hurry! The same currents are there in life, and if you wish to rest on your oars or paddles, don't do it in the middle of a strong current such as your second year at university. Remember, the rests you take on the river must be carefully picked to avoid the currents. So must be the rests you pick from studying.

It would seem to me that an annual seven months of honest endeavor is not too much to ask of anyone. If it is, and all you graduate with from university is a D–average, then you are in for a rude shock when you come to join our company. We demand eleven-and-a-half months of honest endeavor, and A's only are accepted in all our departments.

Of course, our Unemployment Insurance Act allows for the continuance of your five-month annual rest period—but I have not known anyone of your caliber who has ever willingly collected this kind of holiday pay and stayed happy for long.

Remember, if you wish to be a future top business executive, it is impossible to "fly like an eagle with the wings of a wren." You now have four months left to get your momentum back in gear to its former satisfactory level.

Love,

The Other Canoeist

P.S.

It occurs to me that a hard-nosed appraisal of many of those with whom you spent all that rest time during first term might prove beneficial. A few character flaws among this group might be revealed that I hope were all noncontagious.

I would suggest that such an appraisal be made *this* term, for I doubt if many of these friends will be back next year. I also think it might be prudent to select some new friends this term who will be back. They will make better friends in the long run anyway.

First Days in the Real World

*D*ear Son:

Today is a big day in your life. Having accomplished twenty years of schooling, the time has come for you to enter the real world of work. Lots of people do not like the word *work*, for it immediately evokes images of having to get up in the mornings, the repetition of dull acts, little time for play, headaches, backaches, and other assorted miseries. Others are just *a-bustin'* to try their turn at the wheel of fortune and they cannot wait to get started. I would prefer to think you are of the latter school of thought.

Now that formal education has molded your frame of mind, it is time to apply those years of effort to earning a living and your own space in this crazy world of ours. You have one major advantage going for you in that you *know* what you want to do: be a businessman, and a good one. I feel sorry for the many young people who cannot seem to pin down what they want to do to earn a living —and even sorrier for those who *do* know but cannot find a job in their chosen fields. Knowing what you want to do and landing a job in which to do it is a mighty fine start.

Speaking of fine starts, getting to work on time is precisely the right start for your day now. Nothing raises people's eyebrows or tempers faster (including mine), than a person's repeated late arrivals at work. It is hard on the morale of everyone else who has disciplined himself to get out of bed and out to work on time daily. It is particularly hard on the boss's frame of mind—for how is he to feel comfortable about giving you responsibility if you are not responsible enough to get to work on time? Ours is a static starting time. Quitting time—as long as it is after 5:00 or 6:00 P.M.—is up to you. Some firms have flexible working hours, and those who cannot handle our fixed time schedule should probably find a job within one of these companies. I do not intend ever trying to find you at 8:15 A.M. only to learn you usually saunter in around 9:30. If you are part of and dealing with management, you need to be on the same time clock.

You will be joining a group of our employees who have put a lot of their years into moving our companies ahead. (I trust you will be gracious enough to allow a little of their vast experience and knowledge of our operations to permeate your brain.) Although I would see no sense in your trying to reinvent the wheel, I would consider it entirely permissible for you to question any current practices you think could be improved upon or performed in a better way. Just be cautious not to come on *too* strong. Victory often goes to those who bide their time learning more, who *perfect* their ideas before presenting their carefully thought-out plans to management. Should the urge strike you to restructure our policies, bear in mind it need not all be attempted overnight (unless, of course, it happens to be a matter of urgent importance). I *am* for prompt decision making, but untried ideas require careful footing.

You will receive excellent guidance through our training program, and since you will be in the marketing end of our services, I suggest you learn as much as possible about our business before you try testing your salesmanship on one of our customers. Some of them have been with us longer than you have been on the face of this earth. And not only is it imperative that you learn everything about our business, you must as well learn as much as it is humanly possible to learn about our customers and our prospective customers before you even shake hands with them. In a customer's eyes, you only get one chance with your first impression. Make certain you do your homework so that it is a good one! If it is not, you will have to spend at least the next two years trying to get back on a positive footing with that customer. A woeful start.

"Silence is golden," someone said. I concur. And in your case, a pound of listening to an ounce of speaking is about the ratio I would recommend you adopt during this initial period of time with us. I once decided against hiring a salesman simply because a couple of the purchasing agents he had called on in his previous job told me their best description of his approach was "a diarrhea of words." The lesson to be learned? Simple: "It is better to keep your mouth shut and be *thought* a fool, than to open it and remove all doubt." It is hard to dislike a knowledgeable person rather on the quiet side—and purchasing agents especially tend to favor them.

Aside from your knowledge of our business—which must be in your briefcase before you set foot off our premises—instilled in your mind must be the conviction that we offer *better, far better, service* to our customers than our competition does. Only half of our job is *selling* our services; the other half is *servicing our customers to death.*

Otherwise you have to keep finding new customers to replace the ones leaving you due to lack of service. Most inefficient. (Also so stupid it would drive your old man up the wall and around the bend!) Selling is important, but *service* is the name of the game for adding profits to the bottom of our profit-and-loss statement.

Servicing our customers well obviously entails a good working relationship between us and our suppliers—and we have some who service us so well I get jealous of their efficiency in this area. No price cuts by other suppliers or wild horses would ever pull me away from this kind of loyal supplier. I would like to think some of our customers feel the same way about us.

In your early employment days with us, keep this spectrum in mind: at one end, our customer; at the other end, our supplier; and us in between. A perfect spectrum of light, with its colors all blending harmoniously into one another, is a joy to behold. So is a perfect business in its blending of suppliers, employees, and customers.

For the time being, walk softly and forget the big stick. People will be looking at you as the new boy the same way you looked at the new boys at school—sometimes with a bit of a jaundiced eye perhaps?

If all this sounds rather frightening, not to worry; Rome was not built in a day. Moreover, the primary purpose of this letter is not so much to counsel as it is to share with you briefly the pursuit of that oft elusive dream: finding *happiness* in your work. The great writer John Ruskin wrote this in the nineteenth century:

In order for people to be happy in their work, these three things are needed. They must be fit for it. They must not do too much of it. And they must have a sense of success in it.

Your formal education and desire to be in business certainly should make you fit for our work; my observation of you over the past twenty-five years does not lead me to be too concerned you might be doing too much of it; that leaves your happiness at work solely dependent on your personal *sense of success.*

Ambition, initiative, and responsibility, all carefully developed, will make your career a wonderfully enjoyable part of your life. And think of this: the future giants of industry of some thirty years down the road are all starting *their* first days at work today, too. Just as you are. Try not to forget that.

Oh, yes, one other thing: none of those future giants will be terminating their formal training today either, now that they have entered the real world. They will just be *shifting* it—to nights and weekends, with a measure of leisure time thrown in for good balance.

There is a secret desire in a father's heart for his son to do well. I guess that is perhaps why George Herbert wrote, "One father is more than a hundred schoolmasters."

Welcome to the real world of earning a living. I shall have your report card ready at the end of our first fiscal quarter.

Love,

The Headmaster

Integrity

*D*ear Son:

Your report on the loss of the RGM contract was disappointing news. I know how much you counted on it and how hard you had worked for six months to draw it to a successful conclusion. I also know you feel you were falsely and deliberately misled into believing the contract would be yours, and that you now regret having divulged certain private corporate information. Also, in the aftermath, you have unfortunately become very bitter toward the other party, perhaps with good reason, but you must not allow bitterness to discourage you or divert you from pursuing other contracts with your usual optimism and zeal.

As you chalk up a few more years' experience on this planet, you will realize there are few people in whom you can place your trust completely. Therefore, a wise man arms himself with a little ammunition: a little knowledge, or what I call safeguards for those times when he finds himself having to place his trust in another person. Those safeguards can take many forms.

First, you should try to obtain some background about a person you do not know. Most people are creatures of habit and if they do not play the game by the rules, no doubt there is *someone* they have burned or stung along the way—and if for no other reason than even some vague revenge factor lurking in the back of the victim's mind, that kind of information is long remembered. So invest a little time enquiring about the person with whom you are going to conduct business.

Second, you should direct your efforts toward always selling your services on a *personal* level. Remember, the company is a nonentity as far as customers are concerned. People are not doing business with the company; they are doing business with you, personally. If you always treat it that way, customers come to rely on *you*— not on the company—for the success of their contracts. That is not to say, of course, that you should not single out for special attention your excellent staff and superlative facilities and method of operation.

Third, you should look on all ventures at this stage of your life as *experience.* You have forty years to make up the loss of this contract! If you dispassionately examine the events behind this one, you will note one or two things (perhaps more) that you will do differently if you ever again encounter similar circumstances. Wise men learn more from defeat than they do from victory.

My fourth and most major point: you have come away from this with no besmirchment of your character. You did not compromise yourself or the company in your efforts. (If you had, then you would have good cause to hold your head in your hands, and I would also be telling you to bend over for a good swift you know what, where.)

You see, you have what we call *integrity.* Quite obviously, the other guy has none, and I would not give you a plugged nickel for his chances of long-range survival in the business world. Oh, he will stay alive for a while, deluding this person and then switching to bait another. But business is a small world. His lack of integrity cannot help but eventually catch up with him. But, as I have often said before, don't worry about the other guy's integrity; worry about your own!

Owning integrity is owning a way of life that is strong in moral principles—characteristics such as sincerity, honesty, and straightforwardness in your daily living patterns. In the business world, ownership of such characteristics is the lifeblood of any long-term success. In the short run, it is not hard to make a bigger buck by cutting corners on what you promise your customers you will do or deliver. In the long run, though, such tactics are the cornerstones of the big *losers* in industry—the ones avoided like the plague by the *winners*. One of the most important rules is to never give a person cause to say you did not tell the truth, for as Ayub Khan said, "Trust is like a thin thread. Once you break it, it is almost impossible to put it together again."

Once someone has *shafted* you—as you term your recent experience—you might feel like *shafting* someone else. It is only human. Most of us react the same way at such times—as if a little evening of the scales would help your damaged ego. At this point, however, you are in grave danger of losing. Big! Up to this point, you have lost nothing but a contract that was not yours in the first place. The loss of a lot more is at stake if you allow your anger or an impulsive quest for retribution to get the best of you.

Now stop and think about this. How badly will you miss the problems you inevitably would have had to face down the road had you been successful and won the contract? How much will you miss not having to deal continuously with this man who lacks integrity? It is entirely possible the loss of the contract was no failure, but one wonderful blessing in disguise instead.

Chalk one up to experience, to being thankful for discovering beforehand the true nature of a person you might have had to do business with, and all your efforts will have been well worthwhile.

Anyway, that was yesterday. What are you doing *today,* to keep us in business tomorrow?

With love,

Your Guardian Angel

What Is an Entrepreneur?

ear Son:

While in New York last week, we had an interesting conversation going before Mr. Daniels arrived for dinner. Your queries about entrepreneurs were good ones and somewhat tough questions to answer.

My first acquaintance with that rare breed of person occurred during my last years as a cpa at Price Waterhouse. Through your mother, I met a man by the name of John Part. He was about fifty years of age and I about twenty-eight. While attending a few social engagements with him, I found myself intrigued by and drawn to this man, for he so obviously possessed a magnificent business mind.

John Part only worked when he needed money. He would stoke up the brain power and go out and crank up a new product (mostly in the health-care field), or devise some new method or approach to advertising. He was in one of his retirements when I met him, but although he had some left, money was beginning to run a little short.

I wanted badly to see the other side of the business world—see it through a marketing eye instead of a general ledger, so I started badgering this man about when he might next set up another business, and could I join him. He finally decided to go back to work, set a date, and I guess he liked my brown eyes, for he invited me to come along with him. It had to be my brown eyes or my winning smile because few young fellows were as green as I at this stage of my life in the Big City, and there had been a choice of several other assistants John could have picked for his team.

Anyway, my introduction to the real business world, that of "making a buck," got started. By the time John died some six years later, I had had sufficient transfusions of entrepreneurial genes to enable me to carry on the business we had started, which I now bought from his estate. I was not what you would call a rapid learner, nor was I always ahead of the average businessman my age at that point, but I *had* been exposed to John's brilliant creative mind, and I now had a small business to get on with.

The word *entrepreneur* comes from the French word, *entreprendre,* meaning "to undertake." The Oxford Dictionary's definition of the word is: "a contractor acting as an intermediary between labor and capital." Well, I think a few more words are in order to describe this fascinating innovator of the business world.

To me, entrepreneurs are people with great imaginations. They seem to have answers for everything. No problems cannot be solved, no undertakings cannot be carried out. They are creative in their thinking, always seeking new methods of doing things. Their innate aptitude for avoiding the ordinary, the *standard* pathways of the business world, is the very crux of their success.

Entrepreneurs are great observers and students of human nature. John Part did not miss a thing. One of his little pearls of insight was expressed to me at breakfast one morning as we looked out the windows of a restaurant situated on a busy corner in Montreal. Streams of people were hurrying to work—some on foot, others in packed buses. He mused a little over the panorama before us and said, "Look at all those people running to work to earn money; money which they run to spend after payday; money seeking something *we* should be running to bring them in the way of new or improved products or services." I never forgot that. The road to business success is paved by those who continually strive to produce better products or service. It does not have to be a great technological product like television. Ray Kroc of McDonald's fame did it with a simple hamburger.

Many of the ideas entrepreneurs successfully exploit are not their own. An amazing number of people in this world have excellent ideas, but few know how to go about merchandising them. For the entrepreneurs, it is a *natural* ability. They develop ideas from embryo to consumer stage at the speed of a computer, and that swiftly paced modus operandi is one of the main reasons most of them prefer working on their own. Not for them tedious marketing committees, hordes of consultants, and mile-long boards of directors—unless they happen to be such number-one executives as Lee Iacocca of Chrysler, who brought that company back from the brink of bankruptcy. Big companies have their entrepreneurs, of course, but many more are to be found "doing their own thing" without very much ever being heard about them.

I mentioned earlier that lots of people have great ideas but are unable to carry them through to full remunerative bloom. Here is one story I thought you would like that illustrates this point. (It has always been one of my favorites.)

An old man in a farming area outside a city operates a hot-dog stand. Man, does he operate a hot-dog stand! People from miles around have heard about this old man's delicious hot dogs. They have noticed his great big billboards advertising the best hot dogs in the county, and they flock to his roadside diner to try them. He greets them outside when they come, woos them in with his big smiles and joviality, and urges them, "Order two, they're real good." And the people *do* enjoy the very best, most appetizing hot dogs they have ever tasted—nestled in the freshest buns, topped with succulent relish, tangy mustard, onions cooked to a T—and all served by smiling, pleasant attendants. People leave smacking their lips and saying, "I never knew a hot dog could taste so good." As they drive away, the old man waves good-bye and reminds them, "Come back, please. I need the business, and so do the youngsters to get through college." And the people do come back. In droves.

One day, the old man's son comes home from Harvard, where he had graduated with an M.B.A. and a Ph.D. in Economics. He takes one look at his father's operation and says, "My *God*, father, don't you know we're in the middle of a bad recession? You have to cut costs! Dispense with your advertising costs by canceling the billboards. Save labor costs by reducing your staff from six to two, by doing the cooking yourself instead of wasting your time out on the roadside. Get after your suppliers for a cheaper grade of buns and hot dogs. Only serve the inexpensive brands of mustard and relish, and cut the onions out completely. Now, see all the savings you will have for weathering out this recession that's killing businesses left and right?"

The father thanked him, and knowing how *intelligent* his son was with all his degrees, he never for a moment doubted

35

the sound words of advice. Down came the billboards, back went the father into the kitchen, where only the cheapest goods were now being used and only one waitress left to serve them.

Two months later, the son comes home again and asks his father how things are going in the business. The father looks at his empty hot-dog stand, all the cars that used to stop now whizzing by his door, his empty cash register—and he turns to his son and says, "Son, were you ever right! We sure are in one *hell* of a recession!"

You see, the old man *was* an entrepreneur—but only to a point. He knew what people wanted; the only basic component of true entrepreneurship he lacked was the courage of his own convictions. Had he *really* believed in himself, no one else could have destroyed his business. There has to be that stubborn, tenacious streak in an entrepreneur to ensure his success.

The entrepreneur goes with his *gut feeling* when there is an absence of solid evidence to direct him. His gut feel may specialize—in packaging, the medium of advertising, or knowing the type of retail outlet best suited for reaching the consumer of a particular product. He never forgets, by the way, that mail-order and door-to-door selling have made many millionaires. (Sears and Avon, respectively, are good examples of each.)

He will use available marketing assistance to sell, but unlike many now dormant companies, the entrepreneur *ensures* his success by using them differently. For instance, in a test-market program, he himself might journey to the test-market area and personally study the faces, the expressions, the comments—both positive and negative—of the test-market customers exposed to his new product or services. One fellow even went to the

36

extent of taping the customers' remarks so he could study them more thoroughly—much the same way some coaches review their teams' efforts on a video playback. The entrepreneur is shrewdly cognizant that as much as he knows, no one knows it all. He is a firm believer that only fools, convinced they know best what the consumer wants, bypass the test markets. Many a toddling entrepreneur has probably learned that lesson the hard way, but learned it I'm sure he has, for as strong willed as most entrepreneurs are, they are also flexible—an unusual combination of characteristics, but a vital one for success.

Another observation I have made about the entrepreneur is his uncanny ability to measure his risk. He is by nature a person given to taking risks, for he instinctively knows that "Great deals are usually wrought at great risks" (that was said by Herodotus in 450 B.C.). While keenly aware how quickly and easily the most carefully laid of human plans can fail, he does not shirk away from risk. He thrives on the excitement, the tension, the gamble, the fight—and upon conquering them all, spends five minutes relishing his success before charging on to his next hot prospect.

Our entrepreneur is a super think tank when it comes to analyzing the risk areas of a new project. He discerns where it is most likely to break down and zeroes in on the soft areas. If a qualified person or company can help, he will employ them to help him narrow down his risk factors. Undoubtedly, he will also develop an alternate plan in case the one he is using does not work; with always a backup, always an out, he is always financially secure enough to walk away from a failure and start a new venture tomorrow. Bankruptcy courts are not for him. He has been poor too long and detests bread and beans. He has no intention of going back to either ever again.

How does he do it? Well, in various ways, but mostly he rigidly judges how much he can afford to invest in a project. If it is going to cost more than he can cover or if he feels the odds are long against its success, he will do one of three things: he will procure an investment of other people's money and talents; he will sell the idea outright to someone interested in handling it; or he will, if he must, as a last resort, just forget it. An entrepreneur is eminently aware that "It is possible to fail in many ways . . . while to succeed is possible in only one way" (Aristotle said that in 350 B.C.).

Some typical traits of some entrepreneurs frequently "do them in." Not all entrepreneurs are successful. Often they move too swiftly in the planning stages of their projects. In their haste, they cut corners on the quality of their service or product, they neglect to get legal protection for their trademarks or patents or, quite often, they overlook government legislation regarding their new "gold mines." All too often, they do not have sufficient backup for their financial bets, and when they run out of their own funds, bankers refuse to see them, and their investor friends start avoiding them, preferring more stable personalities with whom to conduct business.

Only a fine line differentiates a successful entrepreneur from a successful businessman. They are somewhat the same, of course, but the entrepreneurial personality evinces more dash, more gambling spirit, more daring—and less adherence to the conventional pathways of business. But both must know what buyers want and what trends are occurring in the marketplace. Constant contact with the marketplace together with an accurate assessment of it is a winning combination.

Entrepreneurship sounds most adventuresome and especially appealing to one's ego. But running against the tide is tricky business. Still, I have yet to hear one person I have ever considered a true entrepreneur blame *circumstances* for having caused any of his problems. He is blessed with a short memory for failures and an unquenchable thirst for new ventures. He allows his successes five minutes' worth of crowing and his failures a second's worth of bemoaning.

He tends to go his own way, do his own thing, in or outside of business. Claude Hopkins, a great entrepreneurial favorite of mine, describes his propensity for aloneness this way, in his book *My Life in Advertising*:

I have met other great emergencies, more important than money or business. I have always had to meet them alone. I have had to decide for myself, and always against tremendous opposition. Every great move I have made in life has been ridiculed and opposed by my friends. The greatest winnings I have made, in happiness, in money, or content, have been accomplished amid almost universal scorn. But I have reasoned in this way: The average man is not successful. We meet few who attain their goal, few who are really happy or content. Then why should we let the majority rule in matters affecting our lives?

I have often paused and reflected on Claude Hopkins' statement that every great move he had made in life had been ridiculed and opposed by his friends. I still well remember the many raised eyebrows when, after ten years of studying for it, I left a promising career in accounting to join John Part and his little company with an annual sales volume of only $140,000. Seemed like a crazy move after having audited some of Canada's largest corporations—but our sales of $25 million this year would, I believe, happily indicate otherwise.

You may be interested in the following poem. It is one I have kept over the years for it manifests quite a spark of entrepreneurialism. It was written by a seventh-grade student.

> They look at me and ask why
> I tell them I really don't know
> But every man has a chance to reach for the sky
> I have my own special way
>
> And some day
> Maybe I'll get there
>
> Right now I am on my way
> With many different thoughts every day
>
> I have many problems I have to face
> Some end in good, some in bad
> But in every one
> I never really end up mad
> Sure I have been sad over many of them
> But never, ever, really really mad
>
> I will never let myself get really tied up
> And if I do, I drop it
> Until I may return, not in a folly
> But rather quite jolly
>
> This may not be your way
> It definitely is my way

I hope you enjoyed that little poem because *you* wrote it. Away back then, your independent spirit, optimism, flexibility, brave willingness to bounce back to the fight were all there.

Virgil said, about 25 B.C., "Fortune favors the brave." Be brave with our money, but not *too* brave. I love financial heroes, but not bankrupt ones.

Love,

"I Did It My Way" Ward

Experience

$\mathcal{D}$ear Son:

To your new position as head of marketing for one of our companies, you bring an assortment of talents. First, you have a good brain capable of competing with the world; your achievements at high school and university and in your other jobs within our company have well proven that. Second, you bring a high degree of enthusiasm to your work. And third, you have a sense of measuring the results of your efforts in an evenhanded fashion.

However, there is one basic element you do not at this point in time possess: that of *experience*. Back in your school days, you will recall, experience grew daily by your merely coping with each new day and what it brought until you felt secure enough in what you were doing to measure your results realistically. This new position will develop the same way, but it is vital at this early stage of your job to acknowledge you are light in this key department.

What to do about it? How to work around this big hole and gradually close it in? The man who lacks experience and knows it must first make a resolution to himself that he will not allow this missing factor to inhibit him or

42

prevent him from trying to get the job done. Having done that, it is then crucial for you to take the time to carefully assess each project you are about to undertake —be it the analysis and solution of any given problem, the preparation of a presentation, or anything else on your plate.

First, what and how much data have you immediately at hand? What and how much data is missing? Should you compile more? Once you have all the facts you can possibly obtain, and *only* at this point, will you be at all ready to start thinking about your possible courses of action. Beware of the pitfall so many people fall into— some over and over again—that of not first gathering all the possible, obtainable facts. Many people are lazy when faced with this aspect of their jobs, and they do not work hard enough acquiring the basic data on which their decisions and actions will be founded. You have built enough camps in the woods with me to know that if we fail to provide a firm and level base on which to build, our efforts will certainly fall short of anything resembling a first-class job.

Next is the tendency to want to start analyzing the data, to *get on* with the job, before every conceivably available facet of information has been obtained. Then especially one needs to discipline his mind not to start chugging away in second gear before first obtaining all the benefits of first gear. Think of our camping and canoe trips. Because everyone is always so anxious to get going, are we not apt to leave something behind if we do not—*before* setting out—check my deplored "to do" lists that I go to all that trouble compiling prior to each trip? And it would certainly not be due to lack of experience —but only to lack of properly *applying* our experience.

At the conclusion of step one, the gathering of information, it is great insurance to look around you for a reliable person with whom you can check whether you have missed anything. A colleague in a similar position in another noncompetitive company or your own president are perhaps the two best people to turn to—but there are other good sounding boards.

Now comes the second step, the more exciting one: acting on the information at hand. Here is where the experience factor really counts, because proper interpretation of your data is crucial to your success. As the years pile up and you make your share of mistakes in the business world—as we all do—you will find that 80 percent err in their decision making because of mistaken interpretation of their data rather than because of a *lack* of data. Experience teaches you to first get all your pertinent data together and, second, to analyze it properly. The first requires discipline; the second, years of experience.

How does one go about becoming experienced in interpretation of data? Same as with anything else. By *doing*. But I must hasten to add, it will occur faster and better via careful and thoughtful *analysis* than it will by running with a *gut feeling*.

Upon the completion of data gathering and interpretation, comes execution. No problem for you here; you have already had plenty of experience in this department. The follow-through and follow-up exercised in all your jobs to date as well as during your school years are the experiences you will put to good use now to help you execute your decisions properly. This part of your project therefore should be easy.

But never forget: at sixty-two years of age and with forty years in it, I am still acquiring valuable experience in my field of business. I have simply come to realize and to accept that in certain areas of this business there is still an experience void, still something there to be learned by me through experience—and I remind myself of this each time I tackle a new project. It does not do much for my ego to have to admit to the foregoing, but I rather suspect it helps our profit-and-loss statements considerably.

Shall we both remind ourselves "the woods would be silent if only birds with trained voices did the singing"?

You have all the credentials of a good executive. Experience will make you an outstanding one. But that is something no school, no one but you can accrue for yourself. As you win some, be cautious and steel your mind to keep on learning—from your successes, so you repeat them; from your failures, so you never make the same one twice.

Sincerely,

Your Fellow Learner

Employees

$\mathscr{D}$ear Son:

It was a jolt to learn Mr. Miller left our firm for other employment. It surprised me because during the time I was operating the manufacturing functions of the company, I always considered him a valuable—if somewhat eccentric—employee. Obviously, his eccentricities *got* to you and caused the split.

Amazingly, with all the people in this huge world, no two people think exactly alike. As differently as each of us looks, just so differently each of us thinks—which in itself is a fantastic feat on the part of our Maker. And even more amazingly, despite all these differences, we still somehow manage to marry, procreate loving families, and retain friends and happy, valuable employees.

To me, the older, more successful industrialists of the 1900–1930 era appear to have behaved as if they were half crazy in many instances. Perhaps there are as many tyrants today, but I rather think the majority have changed their attitudes—if for no reason other than the fact that there is now a much more fluid labor market, one that allows for easier changes of employment (except perhaps for those living in small towns). Therefore, there has transpired a narrowing of the spectrum: not so many bully employers now—and not so many hapless stuck-in-their-job employees.

A prudent employer would take the time to analyze the incentives a person might list as his reasons for working—and most importantly, the order in which he lists them. A recent study disclosed that money was number seven on such a list. Topping it was satisfaction in performing the job. Obviously, that good feeling one gets from having accomplished something is still man's best reward for his hard labors. But he also needs to know he is doing his job well, and the major deficiency within management today is the failure of telling him so.

An earned compliment costs nothing, but its returns are immeasurable. Very humanly, when we are complimented, when our efforts are appreciated, most of us will usually strive to perform even better down the line. What a return on the investment of delivering a few earned words of praise!

Now to our case at hand. Unquestionably, John Miller was an honest, hard worker. His few oddball behaviors and opinions certainly never bothered *me*, and I assure you, I assessed them carefully—whether they might even be causing us loss of business. At the same time, as I looked around me to particularly observe, I found it highly interesting how many different, often strange idiosyncrasies most all of us possess—and that despite all of them, we still come together daily, work side by side harmoniously, and constitute a great work force! You see, what we might term oddball characteristics in others, in most cases are nothing more than different views

47

or outlooks, different perspectives than ours about life and living. In short: "different strokes for different folks." It would be fascinating to read the thoughts our fellow workers might be entertaining about your (or my) behavioral patterns or eccentricities—for we do all have them.

Quite obviously then, molding a work force around—or in spite of—the peculiarities within us all becomes a necessity. If we do not, there won't *be* a work force. You must remember, the only perfect employee is not you, yourself alone. Further, it is the output of our business product that counts, not whether someone blows his nose once or twice or a thousand times a day. Unless a person's habits are so offensive or extraordinary that they disrupt others, I see no reason to let that person go off our payroll.

I believe it would be an enlightening exercise for you to evaluate Mr. Miller's reasons for leaving. From what you have told me, his oddball personality finally just got to you. Well, it should be borne in mind that we are in the business of making medicines, not analyzing personalities. The fact Mr. Miller worked with us for ten years and during all that time I heard not one complaint against him from any of the other employees is food for thought.

A sufficient allowance of time is often all that is needed for certain personalities to mesh. In this case, you had been working in contact with Mr. Miller for only four months. Perhaps another four months would have given you a much more positive impression of the man and a new perspective of the situation.

My question now is, did we lose a valuable, trained employee possibly only because your criteria for liking or disliking people is off kilter or eccentric? If we did,

48

then we had better get thee to a head shrinker fast, before you lose our entire labor force for us.

You see, it costs money to train a person for a job: for some positions within our company, a great deal of money. If we are to operate at maximum efficiency (happens in theory only), we must maintain a low labor turnover; otherwise all of our profits will go toward training people if those we train consistently leave us shortly thereafter. Hence, high morale is not only a nice, desirable atmosphere to maintain among our staff, it is a *must*.

In closing, bear in mind you must continually review staff performances—particularly of those who have most recently joined us, to determine whether they are measuring up to our standards. However, a sliding or failing performance by any staff member who has been with us for a number of years should signal a stop sign for you. Stop and think: *Why* has this person's work fallen off? Are pressing personal reasons perhaps behind the decline, which must be taken into consideration if you are doing *your* job? Talk to the person and tell him his work is not what it used to be. Is there a problem we can correct or one we can help him solve? What one single hour of time can do toward putting a person back on his efficient feet again is really astounding. And consider this: that one hour of your time and one hour of his time costs us about $50; on the reverse side of the coin, it will now cost the company $5,000 to train a suitable replacement for Mr. Miller.

Your people are your valuables. Not the bricks. Not the mortar. Not the machinery. Protect this major investment we have in our people by doing your utmost to make them feel that top-rated priority, that satisfaction in the performance of their jobs. If you do, you have no idea what increased feelings of satisfaction you will experience carrying out your own job. And I will smile at the resultant escalating profits.

Sincerely,

Your Fellow Employee

Partnership

$\mathcal{D}$ear Son:

I hear your friend Harold has approached you with a fantastic money-making idea in another industry—one very different from ours. Also, via the grapevine, I was given to understand you are being invited into the partnership because of the prosperous business you and I happen to be in. That leads me to surmise your friends are counting on some of our profits flowing over their way to support their new enterprise. And having carefully assessed all the logistics, Harold and his friends have found all the positive reasons why this company should go to the very top; not a hitch, not one negative or drawback in their plans, I am sure.

Funny thing about human nature and money-making ideas: we summon up all the positive aspects in a matter of a half hour and often live in agony many years for overlooking the negative.

Before you start counting your millions of profits from this venture, allow me to intrude and mention a few things that might save you from having to count your losses in possibly thousands and thousands.

I find myself curious as to why Harold and his two

engineering buddies came to *you* with an invitation to join their expedition. Since theirs is a highly specialized engineering project designed to service heavy construction equipment, I am wondering how *your* particular business acumen is supposed to assist—especially in a field so far removed from ours of making medicines.

Without the slightest intent of any put-down, I must admit the first thought that comes to mind is your family's money—because it seems to me that whenever people come up with new business ideas, they are most adept at solving all their production and marketing problems, but their brains go into deep freeze when it comes to finding the money to get their projects off the ground. And after all has been said and done, it is still money that sets their worlds in motion.

But assuming the idea is sound, has an excellent chance of succeeding, and you do mortgage your soul to get at those millions out there, who is going to manage the business? Obviously, it cannot be you, since you are not technically qualified for their specific type of operation. As well, it would become very hard to increase our efficiency and profits with you spending a great portion of your enthusiasm and time thinking about another business—indeed, ours would more than likely *decrease* in efficiency and profits should you split your talents at this point of time in your business career.

So it appears logical to me that Harold will have to run the business since your new company cannot afford to hire a qualified professional manager at this juncture. Now what do you have on your hands? Harold spending your money, with you at a distance. It could be a fine arrangement *if* Harold knows what he is doing. At thirty-two years of age, he could be one of those rare birds who comes along without the benefit of any business training or experience and instinctively knows how to run a business. But I am inclined to think not. I am afraid the odds are too long against it in this case.

If you invest in ten endeavors like this, one might prosper. The exercise is finding out which one will prosper before you lose all your money on the other nine.

Aside from the fact that this proposed business is not within our industry (which we know something about and *still* make mistakes), and that Harold and his boys from engineering school have no business experience, there is the human aspect to partnerships, about which one usually only learns through experience, most unfortunately very sad.

You will be one of four equal partners, the one putting up the money. Harold will be president, Charlie will sell, and Fred will produce the product. Initially, the efforts of all will be very strong and very dedicated; everyone will be pitching in for all he is worth. Unhappily, as time goes on, most foursomes lose one or two of their members' endeavors to the wayside—even if the business happens to be prospering. It is inevitable. When the going gets tough, those 70- to 80-hour work weeks get to somebody—or somebody's wife—and in jumps "the beginning of the end."

"That damn Charlie takes $200, three-hour lunches daily; and I'm here working my ass off!" "Why should *I* work tonight? The others aren't! And 75 cents of every dollar I make goes into *their* pockets!" Then will come the classic one about you: "Why should that bum get 25 cents out of every dollar we make when *he* doesn't contribute a *damn* thing!" Memories can be very short. Your financial contribution to get the company off the ground will not be very long remembered with robust gratitude. You will discover only too soon that your partners' primary interest is asking, "What are you doing for us today?"

Now if you are hell-bent to go ahead with this partnership, let us assess a few avenues of procedure that might vastly reduce some future agonies. One major advantage you have is knowing each of these fellows very well—their honesty, intelligence, and degrees of diligence. That is a big plus! In my opinion, you should discuss with them all the foregoing negatives; the costs, sacrifices, and realities involved in working long tedious hours; the struggles you must be prepared to face— because, unless this new business is very different from most, only gruelling efforts will see you prosper. Tell them in *writing* so they will at least respect you for having warned them if it does all sour down the line.

Next, let us give some serious thought to the divvying up of the partners' shares. Harold appears to be the key man, along with yourself. Charlie and Fred are necessary, but not leaders. All will wish to own some of the business. (How else would each count all those millions of profits?) Well, there are prudent ways of keeping everyone happy. Harold will probably buy the idea that you and he should own a majority of shares—say 80 percent, split down the middle. So far so good. Now your hard nose had better harden up even more if it is to avoid getting bloodied later. You must tell Charlie and Fred their ownership is going to be 10 percent each. Friendship must *not* enter the picture at this stage for in business it can be a devastating investment except in some very rare circumstances. Sweeten the pie by offering 30 percent of the annual profits before tax to the three: 10 percent each. Now each partner has *two* incentives going for him: a *share of ownership* (an ideal that fades fast since it usually does not put much money into your hands until you have become prosperous and have repaid your business borrowings, which normally takes a very long time), and *profit-sharing* paid out each year, the tangible dollar-in-the-hand payments we all look forward to for our expended efforts.

To avoid some possible future hassles, sit your three partners down *now* with your auditor and lawyer, and work out a basis for evaluating your shares annually. Nothing short of a divorce is as messy as trying to dissolve a business partnership with someone who has taken the view his shares are worth a good deal more than is fair to the remaining partners. So make it a rule that the value of the shares be set out annually in the event someone wishes to sell his shares down the road. This way he will know exactly where he stands financially if he does entertain ideas of leaving the company.

Not so "incidentally," since it is your money fuelling the business, insist on *your* auditors and lawyers acting on behalf of the business. It will give you some control over your money and over the way the partners handle it.

Our business partnership has flourished because of hard work and love. If you proceed with this new venture, I sincerely hope you will find a good measure of both within your new partnership. And might I add, "Nothing ventured, nothing gained!"

Affectionately,

Your Partner

On Delegating

$\mathcal{D}$ear Son:

The late hours you put in at the office last week preparing cash-flow projections for our companies was a good piece of work. Considering our banker's short notice of his need of these figures to transact an increase in our bank line of credit, he should indeed be impressed by your swift cooperation and compliancy.

However, it bothers me somewhat to see you preparing this work all by yourself. When I asked you about this, your reply was that you could do it three times faster, alone, than with others trying to help you. Perhaps this is true, but the hitch in that kind of thinking is that you will still have to be doing this type of work ten years from now if you do not, at some point, take the trouble to teach someone else on our staff how to do it. As well, of course, should you be sick, or away, or tied up with other pressing business matters when such work needs doing in short order, you will undoubtedly find yourself in a quandary, and more importantly, so will the company.

Which brings me to the subject of this letter: delegation. I don't know how many times over the years people have asked me, "How do you manage to run all these companies and still leave yourself a couple of months' free time to pursue flying and the joys of Mother Nature?" My answer has always been the same. "Because I have highly competent executives looking after my businesses on a day-to-day basis." Simple answer, you say? Well, yes, it is simple, but you would be amazed how few people in business train subordinates to higher competency levels so they can turn some of their responsibilities over to them. Why so many avoid delegating to the people working under them is a mystery to me. Is it lack of trust, sheer stupidity, or is the main reason, perhaps, fear that the other person might do a better job? Few are brave enough to say it, but I wish our executives knew how much I value being told a job was turned over to someone else because he or she "will probably do it better than I." And if it's "better than *you* or I," (meaning *me*), I am even more enthusiastic and impressed.

I know of no faster way of improving our businesses' worth than by delegating to every willing and able body as much as he or she can handle—and then some, for as each person's work capabilities grow, so will our business grow. Conversely, stifling any deserving individual's growth is tantamount to stifling your company's growth.

Homer, about 700 B.C., had this to say about delegation:

You will certainly not be able to take the lead in all things yourself, for to one man a god has given deeds of war, and to another the dance, to another the lyre and song, and in another widesounding Zeus puts a good mind.

Again, "different folks—different strokes."

The first precept of sagacious delegation is a careful,

in-depth assessment of your personnel's talents, ambitions, and desires. Given the chance, most people will surprise you with what they are capable of achieving. And you can bet your bottom dollar, the day they're assigned their new responsibilities, they will be walking ten feet tall. With or without a raise in salary, there is no greater thrill in business than being singled out for more challenging and stimulating work—except, perhaps, that of your satisfaction in having delegated the new roles and your observation of each person's success within them.

Now for the second precept. Permitting your staff to assume more important duties entails something you probably never thought of doing: teaching. Simply and fundamentally, putting together a set of tough, competent executives and a dedicated, strong staff requires teaching. The most successful businessmen are often extremely good teachers. That includes preparing a good format, patiently allowing time for it to be digested, being supportive, and spurring your students' potential to its greatest heights.

Once you have made your selection of people and prepared your training program, the results of these efforts should be new people doing at least part of your old jobs. Now your key to ultimate success is the development of a system of control over all the realigned duties. This means establishing a method of communication between you and your personnel whereby you will be kept posted, up to date, and on the alert to spot trouble areas or correct a mistake. Above all, maintain a confidence in your heart that your trainees can and will do their new jobs well. *Your* new job is to help them over the rough spots.

When you reach this golden plateau, you will be collecting your pay for what you are *supposed* to be doing. You are here to organize, lead, develop, inspire, and visualize new vistas for us to tackle. You are not here to sit around either doing or supervising repetitive chores that require some, but most assuredly not *all* of a good leader's time.

Having mulled over the foregoing, I cannot help but conclude that any executive who cannot or will not delegate to those under his supervision must indeed fear his own capabilities of handling his responsibilities. If that executive works for me, he has a good cause to fear for his job! Each time he fails to develop another person, he succeeds in promoting dry rot in the foundation blocks of my business. Undetected dry rot spreads quickly and brings many a fine building toppling down, and I do not intend to allow it a foothold in any of mine!

In providing people the opportunity of proving their mettle, you are invoking one of the least understood tenets of effective leadership. One of my constant, secret, and burning desires in business is to uncover as many bright lights hidden under bushels as I can find; to set loose untried, latent, or repressed talent of any "waiting for a break" who, once associated with me, will try their damnedest to fulfill their aspirations. I know I have said it before, but it is worth saying again: "Build business around people, not people around business." As Virgil said way back in 50 B.C., "We are all not capable of everything."

So—no more late nights doing what others can and should be trained to do. It will bolster both your department's strength and morale, make you look good to the boss, and the kids won't be asleep when you get home at night.

Building a business is like trying to build a pyramid

—in reverse. You are the top stone. How many sturdy, supportive levels of stone eventually form the foundation beneath you depends on your ability to select, train, trust, supervise, or promote the members of your work team. It's a pity how many a businessman fails to grasp this, fearing it might jeopardize his own lofty (soon to become shaky) pinnacle. I don't know about you, but I sleep well at night knowing the base of my pyramid is solid (a base of which, of course, you form a mighty cornerstone).

About 2600 B.C., in Egypt, Snefru built the first true pyramid. However, it was left to his son, Khufu, to build the *ideal* one, the Great Pyramid at Giza. Keep building your pyramid and make it the ideal one, too.

Love,

Snefru

The Fine Art of Negotiation

$\mathcal{D}$ear Son:

Thank you for your compliment on my having obtained that new contract for us with the European firm. It was not without its moments of frustration but, all in all, if I may say so myself, it was a rather good example of applying the basic techniques of negotiation.

On the way home, I kept thinking to myself how much our businesses depend on our utilizing the tenets of mediation. We perform them routinely, yet seldom do we sit back and assess exactly what they are.

We negotiate with customers, employees, suppliers, banks, real-estate agents, and whether we realize it or not, between ourselves. Having experience in business is crucial, but the ability to parley effectively ranks not too far behind.

Why are some people more adept than others in this important area of business? I believe I can capsulize my opinion in a simple formula. It is:

$$F - E = S$$

FLEXIBILITY minus EMOTION equals SUCCESS

A person who is inflexible in his business dealings had better have a monopoly on what he sells, for people tire of wrangling ad nauseam and won't, if there are other avenues to pursue. Flexibility is nothing more than being able to read the intensity of the other fellow's desire and then bending to it as much as one might have to in order to reach a successful conclusion. It's somewhat like a tree in a windstorm; it bends but seldom breaks, then stands taller than ever the day after the storm.

Now for part two of this formula: emotion. Often this is much more difficult to harness than flexibility, be it your own emotion or your adversary's. I would like to have a dime for every contract that was lost because of emotion. People so often tend to dig in their heels on the most ridiculous of points—usually only to prove that they are not going to be pushed around by anyone. If you need proof of this, look at the work load of our courts and lawyers with respect to civil actions. Cases are backed up for months, the courts full of people who cannot negotiate agreements between themselves. One or the other side has remained inflexible, unable to suppress excess emotion or evaluate the other side's position objectively. Thus they must endure the often very high costs involved in securing the "cold neutrality of an impartial judge."

There are three rules to follow in practicing the fine art of negotiation. One: conduct a fact-finding mission. Gather all the information you can on the other party's position, and match it with your own data. Many negotiations fail right from the start because of a lack of facts. In the words of Benjamin Disraeli, "Ignorance never settles a question." Do your homework. It will ultimately make or break your case.

Two: study the information you have culled and weigh each point on a scale of one to ten. Try to weigh the points two ways. First, define *your* assessment of each. Secondly, put on your opponent's hat and try to weigh each fact from his point of view. Understand where the other guy is coming from.

With enough study, you should be able to draft a chart, labeling your facts in the order of their particular importance. For example, delivery of a product might rate a 2 or an 8; price might range as widely on your graph, depending on the competition, your measurement of the supplier's quality, and any other factors that might come into play.

Three: divide a page in two and, from your chart, list all the negotiable points on one side and the points over which you will not budge on the other side. *Keep this latter side short.* List too many here, and you will have cornered yourself into an inflexible role.

You are now ready for a successful outcome of your negotiations. It might take several meetings to iron out certain issues or to provide required information over which you might want to return to your office to ponder, but nine times out of ten, your careful work will culminate in total success. When it doesn't—that one time out of ten—no doubt the muted mutterings from each side of the desk might very well resemble these sentiments of Heinrich Heine's, long ago: "Ordinarily he is insane, but he has lucid moments when he is only stupid." These are the impasses, by the way, during which emotionalism will want to steal center stage. Make sure yours remains in check, well to the sidelines.

Another dogma of successful negotiating is this: do not put two people together to work something out who do not like one another. It portends disaster from the very start. On many an occasion I have asked the other side to please exclude a particular person from our discussions because, putting it diplomatically, our vibes clashed. People who like one another respect one another's views and opinions—and therein lies the secret to keeping emotionalism where it belongs in business: *outside* the conference-room door.

Seldom, if ever, will all of your requests be met, so remember to wear your flexibility fatigues on battle day. And when you find yourself entangled in a particularly tough tug-of-war, try remembering François, Duc de La Rochefoucauld's words: "Quarrels would not last long if the fault were only on one side."

Father Time can lend a hand, too. Sometimes there is every good reason for allowing a span of days, weeks, or even months to pass before attempting a reconciliation or treaty. It lets the dust settle so everyone can view more clearly the issues at stake and perhaps reevaluate original conceptions or misconceptions. A time lapse allows for emotions to subside, too. More than once I have let a problem simmer on the back burner for a while, knowing that my learned colleague was doing the same. On such occasions, though, I have always tried to be the one big enough to pick up the phone first, extend an invitation for lunch, and suggest that *together* we try to break the loggerhead between us.

There is one additional thought to store in your mind. Situations do and will arise wherein you find yourself forced to accept the other fellow's inequitable terms. Your back will have been pushed up against a wall, and if for no reason but to clear the matter off your desk, you will find yourself settling for his biased conditions. Naturally, you will feel you lost the game at such times, and maybe you did—but my experience has been that never, on the next go-round, did that person not try to make amends for what he knew had been an unfair settlement. Funny how even the toughest good businessman usually has a conscience.

A note of caution: however extreme a disparity might arise during any of your negotiations, if it is at all possible, try never, never, *never* to allow the matter to get into the hands of the lawyers. Get all the legal advice you want while gathering your information, but only as a last recourse should you allow the courts to settle your dispute—only when you have utterly and painstakingly exhausted every other conceivable method of settlement. This is one of the toughest lessons to learn because, feeling cheated, it is so human to react impulsively, to want to "take the matter to court and let the law settle it."

One man owed me $15,000 that I could not get out of him, so I sued him. My legal bills rose to $8,000, and still I kept after him. I ended up collecting not one red cent for all my efforts. My doggedness cost me $23,000 instead of the $15,000 loss I should have settled for in the first place. Reason? I had not bothered to do my homework (rule one again) or it would have been clear to me right from the outset that the man just did not have the funds to pay me and was heading for bankruptcy. Emotion made a small man of me in that case.

As I look back on the incident, I now can see the even bigger blunder I made in neglecting my businesses while I kept hounding our lawyers to keep after that guy. God only knows how much it cost me to chase a lost cause instead of getting on with the businesses that were making a buck.

Love,

Give and Take Ward

Marriage

Dear Son:

I overheard you telling a friend that you were thinking of getting married. I had to chuckle as I wondered who the lucky lady might be, since every time I have seen you with a date, she has usually been a different young lady. (I gave up trying to keep track of your social itinerary a long time ago.)

I did not, however, find it a chuckling matter to hear you state, rather computerlike, "Now-is-the-time-for-me-to-get-married." Not next summer or next year, you avowed; it was going to take place now. My eavesdropping turned out to be a little more disturbing than I would have expected. It left me wondering what exactly you think marriage is all about. I rather suspect you feel you should get married now because all your friends are doing it; it is in vogue, so you might as well "take the plunge," too.

Well, Martin Luther said there is no more lovely, friendly, charming relationship, communion, or company than a good marriage. I agree. However, it must be viewed as a hellishly serious commitment! Although marriage is, in a sense, primarily an attraction of na-

67

ture's forces, the binding is what ultimately counts—but that only occurs in its own good time. It is not programmed as a computer is. It does not just automatically happen.

The penalty for not thinking carefully enough about marriage—for not viewing it seriously enough as a huge chunk of your life—is divorce, torn emotions, and, very often, a drained bank account. The torn emotions mostly revolve around a failure syndrome one tends to carry around with him following a ruptured marriage, compounded heavily if children are involved. You have not experienced a father's love for his children. Although husbands and wives unfortunately fall out of love all too frequently, a father never falls out of love for his children. Separation in a marriage inevitably causes devastating agonies.

A very old and learned doctor friend and I once shared a conversation about marriage. He opined that marriage should be viewed and treated as a business; that in marriage, just as in any business, if two equal partners contribute equal input, it will thrive; if one or the other or both parties shirk major responsibilities or repeatedly fail to live up to their end of the bargain, it will, sooner or later, collapse into "bankruptcy."

I have never forgotten that conversation. And carrying his line of thought further, viewed in a business sense, a cold, realistic fact of marriage is that it is probably the most major *investment* to which two partners will ever commit themselves. It is major on two fronts: a good marriage can aid one so much in life that its value is immeasurable; a bad one can cost as immeasurably. The dissolution of a bad marriage costs many a fine family the loss of property and wiped-out bank accounts

68

and businesses, and it often imposes a prolonged, very different, and very difficult standard of living.

Prevalent among young people today seems a far too casual attitude toward marriage. Much too often one hears, "If it doesn't work out, we'll just have to 'split'!" How sad to see such a wonderful, serious state being treated so flippantly. How sad to observe the needless agony that attitude spawns.

There are some people who, for a variety of reasons, get only one chance to marry, and they grab it. I believe some of our best marriages result from such beginnings. Why? Because usually within such unions is not only a feeling for one another, but a rigid commitment to making it work. Fortunately for you, you stand a good chance of attracting several young women's fancies because of the nice character you possess, your quite pleasant personality—and the fact that you look like your old man! If you use all these "blessings" well, you might even stand a chance of convincing one of them to marry you.

With what qualities should your prospective wife be endowed? Well, since you asked for my opinion (I think), here goes: you should select a person who has a warm, likable personality; observe if there are any mean or envious tendencies, for these can create havoc later; a gossipy nature should be shunned; a greedy nature, avoided like the plague.

Since you are going to spend the rest of your life looking at your fair maiden, I hope for your sake that she *is* fair of face. Although in truth, beauty is only skin deep, it is rather nice to look at every morning, especially if it combines beauty of spirit. But *far* more important for your sake, I hope that she is wise, strong, considerate, and true, that she is kind and thoughtful, cares about

such things as values and manners and stimulating conversation, and that she never once misses such special
things as a smile or a child's first step or a glowing sun-
set. But most of all, I hope she has the capacity, as a true
partner, to give and take *in harmony* with you. Don't make
the mistake of picking your partner only for her bubbly
personality or ravishing good looks; enduring marriages
require such enduring qualities as intelligence and integrity, sometimes better known as *class*.

If your marriage is a very good one, it can sweep you
along to greater heights faster than anything else I can
think of. There is nothing like struggling to keep up with
a fine wife's pace to help improve a man's worth in this
world.

There are other considerations, of course, such as:
is she active (not lazy)?; clean (you're not always having
to pick up after her)?; humorous? (ah, now here's a
bonus!). Mind though, if she is intelligent *and* persona-
ble *and* sensitive, surely you must realize you can't have
everything, so allow for some frailties. But if the Big
Three are there, your future stands a good chance of
survival if you work things out together with love and
respect during the inevitable crises you will face—and if
the word "split" is in neither of your hearts or vocabu-
laries.

Do you ever look at any of your friends' wives and say
to yourself, "I wish I were in her husband's shoes"? If
your answer is yes, I would advise you not to see too
much of these people, for you don't need *this* kind of
problem. Think over carefully what you would like, admire, and value most in a lifetime partner, and then go
find your *own* perfect mate. As the saying goes, "Keep
your eyes wide open before marriage—and half shut
afterwards."

Incidentally, if during your search you discover a rare gem, remember, "Faint heart ne'er won fair lady." But pursue the fair lady's hand with some careful planning from the head as well as from the heart. The latter, unbridled, can play all sorts of weird tricks on you. You could find yourself tongue-tied, spilling your soup, bumping into things at the damnedest times or losing your appetite for no good reason at all. So keep a rein on it if you can, at least until you have some measure of how you are being received by the other party.

Women like a thoughtful man. Bear it especially in mind when that very special someone comes along—if you want to see her again past your first date. (A footnote: maintaining this thoughtfulness throughout your next fifty years or so will help all manner of matters considerably.)

Once having "tied the knot," I highly recommend you allot family time and business time in wise proportions on your mental time clock. Alloting too much time in either direction can be unhealthy—and be especially wary that the business side does not far outweigh the other right after the honeymoon. Chasing the almighty buck *is* our business, but if we cannot put bread on the table by pursuing it between 8:00 A.M. and 6:00 P.M. five days a week, we are in the wrong business.

John Dryden wrote the following epitaph intended for his wife:

> Here lies my wife: here let her lie!
> Now she's at rest, and so am I.

Funny? I guess. Still I cannot help but hope that neither you nor your wife ever find cause to harbor the same kind of sentiment.

If you try following through with most of what I have

just said—and if you have the Good Lord and a lot of luck on your side—chances are you will have a happy marriage, something too few people have.

Love,

Cupid

Business Expansion

*D*ear Son:

I have read with great interest your plans to expand our company by some 75 percent in one fell swoop. For someone with but three years' experience in this industry, you certainly are generating some sparkling big plans. That is one very ambitious road ahead that your creativity has mapped out for our company—but I am at a loss to understand why. What has triggered all this foresight, since we are not even operating at full capacity —only at 80 to 90 percent of late? Normally a company can crank up to 120 percent of regular capacity in a business such as ours without imminent need of expansion, but, unless my memory fails me, on only two occasions did your sales efforts tax our capacity to this extent.

The primary statement of your thesis is that our competitor gets far larger orders than we do, chiefly because he has the equipment we haven't to handle such volume. Interesting point. But I know something of our competition and where he sits. First, his business is vastly different from ours in that he offers several major services that we do not. We do not because I have never chosen to enter certain fields of packaging that I consider are rather muddy. Large orders must be replaced with other large orders—and in this particular speciality, I do not envy this competitor's plant investment. There have been significant indications in the marketplace recently that this special form of packaging is falling out of favor with the consumer—ergo, no upward trend can be expected by our competitor even though, for the time being, a good volume is still being maintained. Check a little more closely the types of packagings in which most of our customers are bringing out their new products; you will discover there are three we can bid on, to one on which we cannot. Not a bad ratio.

The expansion of our business has recently been running at about 30 percent per year. We have, in my humble opinion, been about as greedy as one should get. Any good businessman needs *some* length of a greedy streak in him to keep him sharp—but there is no greater or more unhappy business disaster than stepping into the ring of the supergreedy.

We shall never be able to expand our business functions at a much faster rate than at present due to a variety of reasons—and before you think I am being ultra conservative or chicken on this subject, I want you to consider my current problems as president (leaving off your marketing hat for a moment). At our present rate of growth, the purchase of new equipment and plant expansion eats up virtually every cent we make in profit after taxes as well as the amounts I wriggle out of the bank manager. Considering our bank debt goes higher each year, we are not exactly lying still in the stream. The repayment of this borrowed money plus the interest payments will require some *years* of work—so no relaxing on the oars in the marketing department, please.

Once over the financial hurdle of being able to make

enough money to cover our investment debt, there looms the problem of training new people to ensure the products we put out are consistently of the same high quality we have always produced. No doubt you will recall your conversation with me the first day you joined our company wherein I stressed that our success to date was due to a number of reasons—but at the very top to me was our insistence on high-quality workmanship. It is not enough to buy more space, bring in more equipment, and rev it up. You must as well have the compounders, the mechanics, the foremen, and the efficient general staff to *work* on these new lines. Else you could lose my shirt—and yours, too—in about six months!

We added 15 percent to our staff last year and most of the new people were as green as your lawn on the 1st of June. Experienced help in our industry is hard to come by, and I cannot help but feel suspicious about any guy who approaches us saying he wants to leave one of our competitors for this or that or most any reason. If our competitors were running sweat shops we would have more than one person every now and then knocking on our doors for employment. No, my instinctive opinion is that this fellow just cannot fit in at our competitor's for some reason or other—but in any case, I would sooner train our own people, in our own methods, from scratch. It *is* hard to teach an old dog new tricks. Also expensive.

There are some businessmen who hold to a theory that sounds rather negative in today's world of ever-building, bigger and better. It goes something like this: once having developed a business to a successful profit point, you have obviously overcome the major hurdles of covering your debt cost and all the attendant agonies of building your business; you have gone through the roughest and riskiest times during the building of your business—when the loss of a major customer, a key employee or two, or a rejected product batch could have done you in. Now you are not going to budge. You will not expand because it is too comfortable sitting back, feeling safe and content that you now have the business at a level wherein it could survive one or two of the aforementioned downturns.

One must take into account that every time a major expansion is undertaken, it is almost like starting all over again. You have to *dig up* that required extra business and *keep* it. Then you have to earn a lot of *profit* on it to pay for the expansion—and the headache tablets management will undoubtedly need along the way.

Some businessmen choose to adhere to the principle of continual growth done at a pace that never puts the company out on a limb. This requires a tight rein on your ambition—plus my motto, "Do not get too greedy."

Does it come as a surprise that some people have been unfortunate enough to have lost their businesses because of expansion? It happens. Very few have the heart, the patience, or the wherewithal to rebuild from scratch—mostly probably because money lenders have become wary of the unfortunate fellow's business judgment. "Once bitten, twice shy."

It would seem prudent to me to hold to what we know and build at a pace that is comfortable to us *and* to our bank manager. It is a little terrifying to me (and you must admit I do not terrify easily) to think of undertaking a major expansion simply so we can bid on business our competitor has. He *is* competing for the same work we are, but we are not competing for his specialty. Indeed, *our* specialty should be getting orders away from his salesmen that our firm can readily handle.

How about expanding your marketing ideas along

these lines? I will gladly increase my own working hours and pitch in to ensure delivery dates on all the new business you bring in. We will also guarantee our usual high-quality performance to keep all your new customers coming back. As I said earlier, we are only running at 80 to 90 percent of capacity. We could handle it!

And keep sending me your ideas! Without them, we would grow stale in our thinking. And by the way, I have no hangups about your running this train at 120 miles per hour; I just want to make sure the track is clear. Derailment can make one hell of a mess!

Love,

" *Chicken* "

Money

*D*ear Son:

Our accountant asked me to authorize a few bills recently that somewhat raised my eyebrows—"somewhat" meaning close to the ceiling! A few of your expense accounts look like you have been entertaining royalty, yet I know there is not an ounce of business for us in any castle. Then again, perhaps some of your guests consider themselves royalty and demand such lovely evenings on the town. But, all sarcasm aside now, what I am more interested in knowing is whether you have developed a touch of royal spending all by yourself.

You have a number of admirable characteristics about you (besides our money) with which to impress people—customers or friends—but if you are nurturing thoughts of trying to improve your God-given image by turning into a Big Spender, you had better read on.

There are two uses for our money: to invest it for our business and look for that return, and to spend it for happiness—whether the return is a nice piece of furniture to look at over the years or even a hangover on some of those "days after." What is not a proper use of our money and would perturb me most would be spending it to try to impress people.

First impressions *are* important, and for a new customer it is rather pleasant to "lay it on" a bit at a nice restaurant. However, once our customer has seen our plant and you have bought him that $100 meal, you should now be on firm enough turf to be able to discuss business with him. You cannot keep emptying out your pocket (and mine) every time you talk to him.

Then there is this to consider: if you give our customers the impression you are a Big Spender, you might turn a lot of them *off*. It could not help but cross their minds that what you are spending are the profits from the business *they* have given us—and if it is in too grand and glorious a manner, it could also not help but cross their minds that maybe our prices are too high. Before long, they would be looking harder and longer at our competitors' virtues—and your cat-and-dog battles to keep their business would surely ensue shortly thereafter.

It is important to look prosperous, but not wantonly prosperous or like a fool who wastes money. Funny thing about most businessmen: our business is making money —it is even a preoccupation with many of us, but no matter how many millions we might acquire, anyone who squanders it is deemed a fool; a person with whom no one wishes to do business. You have probably heard the old axiom, "A fool and his money are soon parted"? It is accurate.

What I consider one of the many blessings in my life, you have so far missed: being poor. I was born that way and managed to survive a considerable number of years without a pot to you know what in and hardly a window to throw it out of if I *did* have the pot. However, during those years, there was a particularly outstanding millionaire in our town, and it was observing this millionaire that really turned on all my juices. I liked everything I saw; his house, his car, his clothes, and the fact he was always at the top of the donor lists during any of our town's charity drives. As I grew older observing him even more closely, I began hearing things about him—especially how he made his money. I was told he was a rather difficult fellow to work for, very demanding, and that he squeezed the last penny out of every ten-dollar bill he ever made. A lot of people called him "tough and stingy," but in looking back on it now, I realize it was all untrue. The name-callers were but envious of his success —living in their never-never lands and dreaming how they would spend his money if they had it. My mother used to say, "Look after the pennies and the dollars will look after themselves." That millionaire must have known my mother, because that was precisely all he was doing.

But, sir, I can tell you, in that town that man lived the life of a goldfish in a bowl. Everything he did was everybody's business. His goings and comings were everyone's topic of conversation—reviewed and chewed over by all the local gossips and then pulled apart some more. But I noticed at church socials how fawning and obsequious these same people were to him—all smiles and compliments on what he did, how he looked, and what a great, successful businessman he was. Didn't fool him for a minute. He graciously accepted and thanked them all for their kind remarks and in like turn, complimented *them* on their hats or mustaches or the good food they served. He knew exactly the kind of comments or downright hogwash his money provoked behind his back— and he could not have cared less. He simply went out every Monday morning, cranked up the mill, and made some more.

The point of all this? Having money can be a treacherous affair. It can surround you with false friends and drown you in a sea of vest-bursting empty compliments. Having developed most of my friends before I made any money to speak of, there is no need for me to heed my own words now nearly as much as you—born with that little silver spoon in your mouth—should. Beware of strangers *or friends* bearing false gifts of empty words.

Part of everyone's human nature (at least of a great many of us) is to be drawn to someone with money and to desire to become that person's friend—almost as if that in itself provided some sense of security. Lots of people will want to be considered part of your group of friends—some sincerely, some not. You better bloody well be on the lookout for those dying to be in your circle of friends only because of your family's money. On the other hand, you would be well advised not to overlook those kind of honest, down-to-earth people who, so fearful you might misjudge their genuine offer of friendship, tend to draw back and keep a reserved distance from you —even declining to send you a nice invitation to something they would love you to attend that you might equally love attending. These are valuable people worth treasuring. Make sure you put them on your invitation lists *first* so they can feel comfortable about asking you out in return. They hold you in awe. Why, for heaven's sake, I will never know—except that it is just old funny Mother Human Nature and plain old *money* at work again.

Incidentally, one sure fire, fast way to lose a friend is to comply with his request for a loan. That is a no-no. Far better, if you do become aware of a close friend's financial difficulties and you feel he could use some help, *offer* it. Those to whom you offer your help with a loan are usually the ones who will repay it and remain your friends. Inevitably, you will drop the friends who ask you for loans. There are banks to turn to for this service. And if you're thinking this sounds like some funny scale for measuring the quality of your friendships, you're right. It *is*. One that has worked over the centuries.

You must know by now that money does not "make a man." I think it was Themistocles back about 500 B.C. who, when asked by two suitors—one poor, one rich—for his daughter's hand, chose the poor man over the rich because he was the right man for her. Good thinking. He chose a man without money, rather than money without the man.

I take some pride—very little, mind you—in having started the businesses from scratch and making them prosper. Since you joined us when they were already well on their way, your pride will come from building them bigger and better.

Whenever you feel like a big shot though, it had better be due to your having just added a new dimension to the businesses—else I shall have cause for getting out the ole sledgehammer and pounding your chest back in to an "I am a regular person" size. Now that is not to say you should deny yourself all opportunities of crowing a little after a success or two. Just do it *quietly* with one or two close friends. That way, should matters reverse, you will only have to tell those few friends about your failures. If you have not boasted to the world about your successes, neither do you owe it knowledge of your failures.

As I have already mentioned, a lot of people envy

82

people with money. I know a little about that feeling because I have been rich, and I have been poor—and I want to tell you, being rich is better. But it is lonelier, too, and tougher to keep your true friends or develop honest and loyal new ones.

Money is a personal subject, so keep it that way. Treated well, it certainly can result in a greater enjoyment of life, for it is a means of seeing the world, of seeing and owning many of the wonderful, finer things made in this world.

A smart man can become rich, but many become rich and foolish (or their wives do). That is why you will now and then hear about so and so who used to have money but lost it all—usually because of poor investments, or because he spent it all without a single thought for *tomorrow*.

I don't know why I am even mentioning the following point to you since you certainly have never indicated any leaning in this direction, but money *is* to be enjoyed and not kept stashed away like some miser's hoard. And if a reasonable portion of it is spent for happiness, don't start worrying over it (like your mother sometimes does) for no one should have to remember or account for *every* cent he has ever spent.

With respect to our businesses, there are a few cardinal rules to bear uppermost in mind. The first dollar you make is like a seed. Planted well, and with some good help from the Good Lord, it will grow, and the following year you might reap two dollars. Remember, it is a very long way to that first $100,000—usually much longer and much more difficult to travel than to your second million.

Just like your seed, money also grows. So does your credit, and for certain right projects, we need our line of credit at its highest if we are to move ahead rapidly. It is tough to borrow a dollar when you only have one; it is relatively easy, when you already have a million, to borrow a million when it is needed for those bigger deals or a more efficient plant and equipment.

Making money is a slow process; losing it can happen quickly enough to make your head spin. Therefore, once you have found that right track for making a dollar, don't start playing around with your winning pattern just for variety's sake or a change of scene. The ways to success are few and far between. Once you have found a prosperous route, stay on it. Seems to me that many who manage to make money in one business tend to regard themselves as some kind of geniuses, and off they venture into far-off fields—completely different types of businesses— often only to lose all they made in their first ones. Most of it is caused by boredom with the first business or by a view of their entrepreneurship so overblown it would sink a dry cedar log.

Need I point out that if you are spending our money at an accelerated rate because you feel we might be accumulating too much of it, I know a few people who could use a hand? Also a few hospitals who have repaired us. I would not want you to feel you are drowning in a sea of dollars—although at the moment it would more likely be a sea of bills, from the look of your last month's expense account.

I do not agree with Timothy of the Bible that "The love of money is the root of all evil," nor with Ecclesiastes in that same fine book, which states, "A feast is made for laughter, and wine maketh merrv: but money answereth all things." Somewhere in the middle there is room for *common sense,* for kindness, hard work, enjoyment, and good times all tied in with having a buck. I hope your genes provided you with a little of each to think about as you spend it.

When next at one of your dinners, parties, or meetings, keep a running tab going on your *reputation*—something far more valuable than any amount of money. Practice a quiet balancing of your personal wallet and a quiet intelligent art in the handling of the company's wallet. Fame and money can be but fleeting moments in one's life; truth and an honest reputation are the stays of a valuable life. No one has ever been able to purchase such ultimate treasures as a good family, sound health, true friends, loyal employees, true love—or true respect.

Yours financially,

Father

Public Speaking

$\mathcal{D}$ear Son:

It was exciting news to hear that one of your former professors has invited you to address his final-year students on the subject of your first years in the business world. He must have thought a lot of you when you were at his university (although I must say your marks would not have led me to think so at the time). Anyway you cut it, though, your pride must have sent three buttons flying off your vest when you were asked—and justifiably so, but now your mind has gotten "back in gear" and you fear you are rather poorly equipped to tackle such an esteemed assignment.

What your observations of the business world are now compared to what they were while you were attending university is something on which I cannot be of much help to you. These thoughts are your own personal property. (My only guess at their contents would be that you might tell your audience you never realized you would have to work for an S.O.B. like your father some day. If that is so, then remind them the business world is full of S.O.B.'s. They are called *bosses,* a term not much used in university circles.)

How well you are going to perform as a public speaker is still an unknown, but some things we do know for sure. For instance, we know you have the first basic ingredient, a mouth; the second ingredient, your mind (at least when I last noticed); and third, two feet on which to stand.

Let's talk about the mouth first. How you send your words from your mouth is very important. Practice your enunciation so you pronounce your words distinctly enough for people to understand easily what you are saying. I have sat listening to speakers with brilliant subject matter in their speeches and lost most of it because I could not understand many of the words or expressions. The speakers' lack of good diction, clear articulation of words, or sufficient volume ruined the gist of what they had to say, since it was virtually impossible to capture.

Prepare your speech *now,* for practicing your delivery will take a lot longer. Start that by reading your speech out loud and ask someone to listen and tell you which words are not coming across clearly enough. If there are certain words you cannot get your tongue around, change them to ones your tongue prefers.

Once you have honed your speech and your diction to the best of your ability, practice standing behind a lectern (the bedroom dresser will do), in front of a microphone. (Use anything to simulate this, but be certain it is not more than six inches from your mouth.) Now deliver your speech to a mirror and practice not moving your mouth any more than six to eight inches from the mike—otherwise your voice will bounce from hard-rock to *Silent Night* volume like a yo-yo, and people will find it very hard to follow what you are saying. Stand evenly on both feet and do not sway or slouch or the motion will distract your audience away from your speech—of which (because it is so dynamic) your audience will not want to miss one word.

The really great orators have one further arrow in their quiver: breathing technique. Take a deep breath and deliver whole sentences or complete clauses of long sentences at *one time*. Do *not*—I repeat, do *not*—start a sentence half out of breath, then run out of breath completely half way through a word or on some meaningless preposition. That makes for terrible delivery. This is the toughest knack to master for anyone interested in becoming a reasonably good public speaker, and it requires constant practice, preferably in front of people. Practicing at home is vital, of course, but hardly equivalent to the real thing, since (unless you are unlike most normal human beings) at the outset of your public speaking, you will feel considerably nervous about facing and addressing crowds of people. But not to worry. Most of this nervousness disappears with experience. In the meantime, just make a concerted effort to control your nerves enough to allow for free breathing. (I had a helluva time with this initially; I found it embarrassing and unprofessional—something you might or might not experience. If you do, all I can tell you is that each new time does get easier and easier.)

Probably one of your best bets would be to join Toastmasters, a group devoted to the practice of public speaking as its reason for existence. It is probably the best type of training you could get because most of it entails the practical experience of speaking before a group of people—in this case, your classmates, all of whom are there for the same reason you are: to learn, practice, and perfect public speaking. I have been told by many devotees of these courses that only thanks to them were they able to conquer their fears and never embarrass themselves on the speaker's podium.

You are probably wondering, as everyone else does, why one gets so damn nervous before speaking in public. Since it happens to the best of us, perhaps it occurs only to reinforce how very human we all are. But whatever the reason, it is to be expected. After all, there you suddenly are, up on a podium with a microphone stuck in front of your face, the spotlight turned on you and you alone, before an assemblage of people waiting to hear what you have to say. For most of us that is pretty unfamiliar territory, pretty heavy stuff. But there are some tricks!

One easy way of controlling a case of shaking knees and a pounding heart is to place both your hands firmly on either side of your lectern. You will be amazed what physical support that will give you. Another little trick is to think of all the members of your audience as friends who are eager to hear what you have to say. After all, even if they are not, they *have* all assembled together for the express purpose of hearing you speak. And still another little trick is to concentrate on speaking to only one person at a time throughout your delivery.

Better than any little trick, though, is this advice from an old friend of mine. You will notice most of your nervousness disappearing after you make only a couple of public speeches if, and it's another big "if," each time you speak, you have the confidence of knowing you did all your homework, you prepared a good text, and you now have something valid to share. Then you have only to stand back and accept those toe-curling, nice compliments from your audience because you have earned them. And once having gotten this far, man, you just know you are over the big hurdle in public speaking. It is a uniquely pleasant feeling knowing you have words people want to hear, opinions or experiences they want to be told about. That is the zenith of any public speaker's goals!

A good man on the podium never talks down to his audience; he does the direct opposite. He makes his audience feel a part of his world, and he respects their interest and intelligence. Moreover, he accomplishes all of this within seconds of his opening remarks, making sure his audience is and will be with him all the way.

As you stand in front of your audience, you will see and sense pretty promptly if your audience is with you. It *ain't hard,* believe me. Either all eyes are riveted on you and not one person lets a cough escape—or lots of persons are coughing and fidgeting in their chairs, whispering to each other, or shuffling papers noisily around. It does not take a genius I.Q. to realize when you have lost them. If this does happen, then give yourself a D for effort and analyze what went wrong.

There is not a greater feeling than knowing you are delivering a good, successful speech—nor a worse one than realizing you are "bombing out." What is the criterion that invariably separates the two? Easy. The amount of hard work and preparation you devoted to the first and did *not* to the "bomb." (A valuable lesson to be learned with respect to *all* worthwhile endeavors in life.)

The smartest of all speakers are masters at learning *while performing* and one of their best methods of doing so is via question-and-answer periods conducted after their remarks. Audience participation keeps the speaker's and the audience's minds working; it provides the speaker with feedback on the pros and cons of his remarks and insight into areas he might have failed to cover or did not cover adequately. It also often sparks dialogue directly opposed to some of the speaker's views, and if his are proven wrong, he and likely a good portion of his audience come away having learned even more than either had expected. That is as it should be, for I believe not one of us has yet acquired all there is to know on this planet—and I often think having open ears and a shut mouth is still the best method of learning.

Some people stop learning the day they leave school. Those ever eager to *do* something or to do *more* with their one time around this earth stop learning the day they die.

Your mother has sewn your vest buttons back on. Don't send them popping off again when you get that first round of applause.

Sincerely,

A Member of Your Admiring Audience

Manners, Attire, and Deportment

*D*ear Son:

Your recent attempts at locating a salesman for our company's services appear to have ground to a halt. It seems to come as a surprise that none of the applicants so far have the least impressed you with their personal attributes. Well, join the club. Neither do many usually impress me. Few people take the time to study the finer points of life that make them appealing to other people. Oh, some can win over the girls one way or another, or some of their buddies perhaps, but when it comes to impressing the boss or a prospective boss, a lot of them come up with a flat zero.

This lack of ability to project one's image favorably is a mystery to me. If one is willing to spend four to six years learning a profession, why not take another week or two and learn a few principles about clothes, manners, and the art of conversation? Even if there has been no formal education, why not learn some of the fundamental rules of society that might readily assist your landing a job in the first place, or moving up the corporate ladder in the second place?

Nothing is more potent in a man's arsenal of attributes than first, knowledge, of course, but secondly, *good manners*. Seems to me a great many people only go half way preparing themselves for the business world. Deportment, as importantly as it might affect one's business career, is seldom seriously considered a category that might require some attention or improvement. In the fourteenth century, William of Wykeham founded two schools, Winchester College and New College, Oxford. His colleges' motto? "Manners maketh man." I feel that motto well befits an educator, for both knowledge and conduct *should* be improved at the same time. Unfortunately, few educators teach both.

Let's examine what manners really are. Are they not simply kindnesses to your fellow men? You start with a "thank you," probably the most universally used good manner in the world, and another nice one, "you're welcome," automatically follows. "Please," though, often gets lost in the shuffle of our day-to-day conversation. If you counted the times you say "please" in a day in relation to the number of requests you make of your employees, telephone operators, store clerks, whomever, I would bet you could increase your usage of the word tenfold. And if you do, pay special attention to the results, for it is my observation that a person's willingness to comply—even the promptness with which he complies—improves dramatically when your request or instruction either starts or ends with a simple "please."

Some manners greatly influence how happily and productively people carry out your directives. Ask and you shall receive; demand and you will get less. If your approach sounds more like a reproach, you will get

93

back a lot less still. Open a door for a lady, hold a door for a man, stand up when a woman enters the room, help a person on or off with his coat—these and hundreds of other such gestures are all demonstrations of *thoughtfulness* to which people cannot help but respond favorably. They are the rudimentary rules of society. They are easy to learn and cost you nothing. And when you may least expect it, observing these rules may sometimes gain you a job, or a promotion, contract, client, or friend.

A common bad manner—interrupting someone while he is speaking—is a conversational habit that diminishes a lot of people's images in my eyes. This is a tactless and frustrating insult to the person speaking. It indicates lack of interest and consideration for the person's views, implies they are not very important. It is usually the habit of a self-centered individual, a person much more prone to talking than to listening—traits neither very appealing or endearing to anyone's heart. While another person is talking, a polite silence is golden, for it displays respect for the other's intelligence and point of view.

Many a person's conversation is limited to one subject: "me." Nothing is as boring or impolite as verbally bombarding a listener with trivia about yourself. On the other hand, enquiring about another's family or fortune expresses concern and caring about the other's existence. While one must guard against overstepping certain boundaries and delving into questions of too personal a nature, asking friendly questions that express your genuine interest in another human being is one of the simplest ways of ingratiating yourself to another.

Becoming a polite, good conversationalist with whom

it is easy to exchange lively, interesting dialogue requires some thought. There is a world full of subjects on which to base a conversation and at least a thousand ways of opening one up other than with a vapid contemplation of the weather. "Is this your home town?" "Where do you live?" "Is it an exciting city?" "How's your football team doing this year?" "Where do you work?"

First impressions are still and ever will be very important—especially when you are looking for a job. It might be the only impression you get to project, so you would be well advised to take full advantage of it. Three physical habits either particularly impress me or completely turn me off, respectively, upon first meeting a person. First and foremost, a firm or limp handshake. Second, looking me in the eye while speaking or listening to me —or gazing out at the steno pool. Third, good or poor posture.

Several people have told me that Prince Phillip, conversing with you in a crowd of two thousand, can make you feel like the only other person there on earth with him. That kind of conversational knack is one young people joining the business world and looking for success would do well to emulate. His is the peak of conversational etiquette—asking intelligent questions, allowing time for you to answer while he attentively listens, responding to what you have to say and pacing the flow of verbal exchange so that you find yourself quickly at ease. If a person can attain a Bachelor of Arts degree, surely he can accomplish something akin to this master's magnificent trait to add to his list of personal attributes. Alfred, Lord Tennyson said, "The greater man, the greater courtesy." I hasten to point out that the courtesy of which he speaks is attainable by all interested, intelligent parties.

Continuing this saga on how a young executive (or anyone else for that matter) might improve the image he projects, let me add a word or two about clothes. The world has all manner of dress—from Eskimos' attire to African tribal clothes. You are certainly entitled to your freedom of choice in what you want to wear in our society. (I am sure you will underscore that, having witnessed my sloppy duds of a Saturday morning.) But when you are being interviewed, or are working in an office with clients and their or your personnel, or are meeting with your suppliers, there is an unwritten law designating the proper attire for today's businessman. That universal code is to dress not to your liking, but to what you know or think is the liking of the person you are meeting. Long hair, shaggy beard, unpressed pants, unshined shoes, and yesterday's four o'clock shadow are a few of the common modes or oversights well known for turning a lot of people off. Of course, you don't have to shine your shoes if you are working in the warehouse, but you had better do so if you work anywhere near the boss's view and you want to keep those brownie points galloping upward on your personal scoreboard.

Clothes don't make a person, it is true, but they do seem to speak for you sometimes. For instance, picture this: you have been invited to someone's home for dinner; the hostess has fussed all day preparing something special; she has set an elaborate table with silver and crystal; she and the host, dressed to the gills in their finery, greet you at their door and you are in your old jeans and a T-shirt that has seen better days. I can tell you, it is a let down for your hostess—almost a slight, considering the trouble she went to all day. Unless you are invited to "come casual," wear at least a jacket (preferably a jacket and tie) when you are asked to someone's home for dinner. It is a lot safer (you can always take the jacket and tie off if you are overdressed) and in a way, it is a compliment to your hosts, for what your attire is saying is that you value their invitation and their efforts to please you. People enjoy associating with people who look clean, well attired, and well groomed, even if they themselves are not as adept as you with style, color, taste, or line. If you have a few extra dollars, investing them in a good-quality, well-cut business suit instead of a trendy sports jacket your weekend buddies might rave over is an excellent investment in yourself. And speaking of visiting someone in their home, if it is for dinner, for goodness sake pick up the napkin and put it on your lap when you sit down, and know the order in which to pick up a piece of the seventeen pieces of silverware that might be confronting you. We older folk are a bit sticky about table manners, and many a junior executive has long remained junior because he did not know the difference between a salad, dinner, and fish fork or between a soup spoon and a dessert spoon on the occasions when he was invited to dine with the boss.

If the boss is scouting from among a few candidates on his list for an executive post, he will most likely dine with the chosen few before making his final decision—so your table manners count on business occasions, too. I remember one company president telling me how a business dinner influenced his final choice between two equally qualified men for a promotion within his firm. It is a rather tragicomic tale. The boss had invited the two young men to an elegant restaurant for dinner. Upon placing his order with the waiter, the fellow who lost out simply did not "start at the beginning." He ordered his main course first, then could not make up his mind about the rest. To the president's well-organized mind, one should order in the sequence food is usually listed on a menu, served, and eaten. According to him, only a disorganized mind would jump to the middle course, order it first, then thrash about hemming and hawing, expecting a confused waiter to sort it all out. The moral of this story? If you don't want anything but the main course, tell the waiter so from the start. It will simplify his day and you might be the fellow who wins a promotion.

When two candidates vying for one position are equally eligible professionally in the eyes of the interviewer, very often what tips the scale the victor's way is either a display of better manners, better choice of attire, better grooming, or a firmer and easier command of conversational techniques. If you stop to consider it, how else could one choose between two Bachelor of Science graduates with equal marks and equal experience in one specific field?

But, back to the problem at hand. Keep searching for your salesperson. If he is going to represent you and me and our business out there, we want someone we will be proud to introduce as our business associate and *to* our business associates. There are people around with all the aforementioned qualities. Trouble is they are few. In high demand, they are snapped up as fast as they appear. But you will know our person when you see him, for he stands well apart and above any crowd. You might try checking with a few purchasing agents who are called on daily by many sales representatives. One of them might have a good tip as to where our well-groomed, well-deported salesperson might be located.

Edward Lucas once said, "There can be no defense

like elaborate courtesy." A very interesting thought. I would change one word, however, to a *sports* term for the young businessman busting to get ahead: in my view, there can be no *offense* like elaborate courtesy.

Thank you,

Emily Post

Bank Managers

$\mathcal{D}$ear Son:

I understand your recent efforts to borrow money from the bank did not meet with success. You might be wondering why I did not offer the contribution of my experience as help with your application. There was a reason. I set you loose preparing this application on your own because I felt it was time for you, at this stage of your business experience, to get your feet wet learning a few things about banking.

Many businessmen take banks for granted—until they are turned down for a loan or their loans get re-called. Funny thing how people underestimate the importance of such a key element in our business circles. I cannot remember how long it took me to realize that in addition to having a plant, equipment, inventory, employees, and customers, I also needed a *banker*. I think it likely was the day before I started in business, probably because I was starting from scratch. You missed that experience, joining us after our banking connections had been firmly established. (At least up until *now* they have been firmly established.)

Maybe, just maybe, was there an *under*appreciation of

the importance of the bank in your *over*enthusiasm about adding another business to our companies?

You knew we had never been turned down by our bankers during all our years in business. Did you possibly rely too heavily on this past successful record and expect almost automatic compliance on their part this time as well?

Your initial reaction to their refusal of your proposal was that of a beaten man. "They're numskulls! They don't know what they're doing! They made a mistake!" Well now, bankers *are* human, believe it or not, and they *do* make mistakes—but I am not so sure they did in this instance when I look over your application and peruse the reasons you gave for wanting to get your hands on their money.

A banker, according to some opinions, is a person who lends you an umbrella on a sunny day but wants it back as soon as it starts raining. Now, there is some truth to that, but he is much else, too. The banker is the only person I know selling something everybody wants. Therefore, he must pick and choose and sift and sort his customers very carefully if he is to keep his bad debts from piling up. He does not loan out his bank's money easily to *anyone*; there are always *some* strings attached. (Some say so he can use them to pull the loans back into his pocket without having to budge from his chair.)

Judging from your application, you were very confident this purchase would be an advantageous move for our company. Was perhaps a slight note of overconfidence responsible for your less-than-well-thought-out report to the bank?

There is nothing like taking a "Hell, they will never go for that!" attitude to instill some deep thinking on your part when preparing for your banker. You might consider such an exercise a waste of time—but the bank manager will make you do it—and you will come to realize he is doing you a favor in forcing you to reexamine your proposed business intentions. Once you do, once you think further about your intended purchase and how much you need to borrow to pay for it, you will find a little of your initial enthusiasm about building a bigger business starting to wane. If it is sufficient to bring you all the way back down to earth, you will then be able to analyze your proposal from a cooler, more levelheaded point of view. If you do *not* and we make a big mistake buying this company, not only will we lose the profits from our present comfortable business, there won't be enough money left to buy all the Alka-Seltzer we will need for our headaches once that new business lands on our desks.

You see, haste in business breeds failure, and while the purchase of another business is exciting, it is also a little like eyeing a pretty girl. You might like her hair, her legs, her good looks—but if the way she thinks spoils it all, how long will she remain exciting to you? So it is with business. What is *not* immediately apparent warrants as much—sometimes a good deal *more*—consideration as does the obvious. "What you eye is not always what you should buy!"

When the bank manager examined the business you are interested in buying, he did not like the accounts receivable you were purchasing with his money. Like my race horses, too old and too slow. The inventory bothered him a bit, too, its rate of turnover being at about the same pace as bodies in a graveyard.

Another thing the banker felt could cause him countless nights of lost sleep was the limited amount of *your* money you were proposing to put into the purchase price. He only sleeps well at night when *you* have the first 20 or 30 percent risk money involved in your mutual venture; that has to be lost first before he needs to start worrying whether his funds are going to go down the drain. I am sure that having no risk money at stake was a nice, comforting thought for *you*; there were to be no nights of lost sleep in *your* bed. Not so comforting a thought, though, for your not-so-friendly banker.

Rarely do sons think and perform exactly as do their fathers, therefore, your rapport with the banking fraternity should decidedly be established on your own, applying your own unique abilities and personality and, most especially, your own money and time. I have cultivated *my* garden; it is time you started cultivating yours.

I would suggest you start by asking your banker to lunch—something you have never done, to the best of my knowledge. For some reason, it is much easier talking to someone over a nice amiable lunch than from the other side of a cold, hard desk. Especially your banker's. Mind though, you are starting with one hand tied behind your back because at this point, although your banker will appreciate lunch, how will he help but notice the begging cap you are now wearing? Would have been easier if you had had lunch a couple of times a year, updating him concerning your business intentions *before* asking him for his money. But, never mind. So you don't have this preplanned benefit riding for you. He will understand because 98 percent of your competition for his dollar usually behaves the same way.

Along about dessert time, I suggest you make it clear you expect and are prepared to put up a good percentage of the purchase price. Your banker should now be about as mellow and receptive as he is ever going to be and he might let you off lightly in this department. It all hinges on how many sleepless nights he most recently lost on similar deals. Therefore your *timing* counts. Some times *are* better than others to approach your banker for a loan. Have a friendly lunch with the *assistant* bank manager now and then. Well acquainted with his boss's work load and schedule, he is the ideal person to advise you when it might be best to extend your invitation to the bank manager. Should bank matters be in turmoil, he will recommend you wait until they are more settled. And you never know, a propitious delay of a week or two —that one factor—might be all that is needed to result in success with a proposal. Another preplanned benefit to be utilized.

Above all, remember your banker is doing you a big favor for free! If, upon reviewing your deal, he turns it down, he has probably saved you from making a big financial mistake. He reviews such deals daily; you and I, once a year or less. As disappointing as it might be not to be loaned the money for a business venture, it is nothing compared to the ensuing disappointment and worry one is forced to wrestle with over a bad purchase of a big can of worms. So listen carefully to your banker's concern about your business. Then try again.

Love,

The Family Banker

P.S.

I would also suggest you meet with the owner of the business you are contemplating buying and discuss with him his creaking receivables and dead inventory. The discussion should result in quite a cost change —particularly if you tell him to keep his receivables and that we will buy only inventory that can be turned over in six months' time.

On Dealing with Government

$\mathcal{D}$ear Son:

Your concern and attitude during our recent plant inspection disclosed a good trait—your desire to obey the law. I, too, wish to obey the law, but as I grow older ever learning, I note that the written law is one thing, the interpretation of the law, something else. You presented our strong points well in rebuttal to the inspector's comments but failed to change his mind. The explanations you gave were sound and valid, and I agree with you that some of the inspector's observations and judgments were incorrect.

What to do now? Well, the first thing to tackle is a review of our case to reconfirm the strengths of our viewpoints. If still satisfied we have substantial grounds for argument on our side, the next step is to appeal the inspector's remarks to his supervisor.

Now I appreciate your concern about taking such a step, your worry that it might antagonize the inspector and result in his being even tougher on us. However, one thing I have learned about our civil service, federal or provincial: they are basically honest, do not harbor grudges, and they do not purposely look for reasons to cause us trouble.

It astounds me how many people in business shy away from presenting their cases to the higher courts within our civil-service structure. It stands to reason that, as within most any organization, the higher up you go on the organization chart, the more intelligence and common sense you will encounter. Still, most business executives, preferring to avoid conflict, accept a government inspector's interpretation as gospel. It is not, and I have had personal experiences to prove it.

One of my best victories was an experience with a sales-tax auditor who was trying to assess us tax on our packaging materials—a levy that would have cost us $100,000 in back taxes and about $75,000 for each year in the future. Well, sir, we took this one on on *two* fronts. The appeal procedure set up was to be utilized in due course. At the same time, we went after our local member of parliament and told him about the asinine ruling that had been slapped against us and how damaging it was going to be to our company. That started the wheels turning politically. And, boy, did they turn, for our member (partly because he was with the ruling party) happened to be carrying quite some weight in government ranks. We then hired Canada's top tax firm. Their preliminary examination disclosed there were good grounds on which to oppose the ruling, so we put up $10,000 to have them prepare the case. It was based on legal precedents that had been set during court cases of a similar nature over the past fifty years.

We now had the government in a bind: our elected official and our lawyers on one side, and the civil servants in revenue on the other. The result? An assessment for

$1,603 for some trivial matters. A far cry from $100,000 for back taxes and a tab of $75,000 each year thereafter!

You see, despite what most people say or think to the contrary, common sense *does* prevail in government. Actually, our politician's efforts won the case for us; we had not even needed the lawyers. But then we will never really know whether the government moved the way it did because of its knowledge of the legal case being prepared for us and our determination to take them to court, or whether the inspector had, in fact, simply made an error in his interpretation of the regulations.

We were out the $10,000 we had spent for the preparation of the case—but failing to win can happen in many different ways, so you have to use all the means at your disposal when you're out there gunning for success. (Kind of like shooting a grouse with a shotgun instead of a .22 rifle: a good spread of *offense* makes *defense* very difficult.)

There are other examples of my having "won some and lost some" battles—with income-tax, sales-tax, food-and-drug inspectors, animal inspectors, and perhaps a few others I can't remember—but suffice it to say, if you have the patience to analyze your case carefully, and you decide you are in the right, pursue it all the way to the senior ranks of the civil service. You will win.

Have no fear of anyone's seeking any type of *revenge* for your actions. If you feel an inspector is "putting it to you," call his supervisor and ask for another inspector. Most senior supervisors will grant such a request provided you have grounds for making it. I must say I have never had to take this measure myself, since the government more often than not sends someone different each inspection time.

You must win your spurs in this arena, so on with the

task! When you win—as I am sure you will, it will be a bigger morale booster than any football game you ever won as quarterback. Right *is* might, but no one wins who does not fight.

I believe it was Francis Bacon who said, "Nothing is terrible except fear itself." Let's not go through life being afraid of government. They are there to *help* us in business and will do so, for they are elected and appointed by the people—and that, my son, is *us*. Admit when you are wrong, but "stick it to them"—and stick to your *own* convictions when you are convinced you are right.

Signed,

Never Give An Inch Ward

On the Principle
of Diversification

$\mathcal{D}$ear Son:

Your comments the other day about the range of companies we own were provocative. So was your questioning of the rationale behind the diversification of the companies within our family group. "Is a company not stronger by confining itself to one field, rather than spreading out into four or five? With diversification, are there not four or five times the people problems, money problems, management, and other problems?"

All my business life I have attempted to ensure, to the furthest extent possible, a financial security that would always *be there*. Toward this end, I opted for diversification of my operations. Now you come along with the same kind of security thinking but proffer it might be better accomplished if we concentrated all our energies in one area of business.

Many would say your line of thought is a good one— the best way to grow; however, let me express a few of my thoughts on this subject.

The very basis of my business philosophy has always been: "Do not put all your eggs in one basket." When opportunities arose to invest in companies with related interests to ours, I always immediately took into account two main considerations. First, did I have enough financial backing to give the new venture a try, and second, did I have the capable, experienced people necessary for the running of it? (The latter being the principle of building companies around people—not people around companies.) If I answered "yes" to both those questions, I then proceeded to ask the other usual business questions pertaining to marketing, distribution, competition, and so forth.

I felt that as long as the new operation had a common link with what I was already doing, I was not taking too much of a gamble—and it did not matter whether it was a vertical or horizontal spread. The governing principle (tendered by Henry David Thoreau) was, "Beware of all enterprises that require *new* clothes."

The reasons for my interest in diversification were twofold. Having been poor once, I had no desire of reliving that experience, so there was the natural tendency to want to protect myself. To me, owning a second business in case the first one failed made good sense. I also observed how slowly businesses are built (especially those in this industry), and that in running one business, my abilities were being utilized but a few hours each day— not ten or even eight, which I wanted to expend. So, since most of my functions were repetitive, I hired good people who knew their stuff to perform many of *my* jobs while I got on with other matters.

It has always been with me that victory has a way of shifting itself from one company to another. My logic dictated that if I had more than one company around, I just might enjoy at least one victory a year out of the group—and that is pretty much the way it has turned out to be so far, with each victory being large enough to cover minor losses or poor profits in the other companies and then some.

One danger in owning a group of companies is that it could "go to one's head," so to speak. One could quite easily start viewing himself as some Einstein of business, fully capable of making any business work and grow. I do grow old, my son, ever learning—and one thing I can tell you unequivocally: the first cardinal rule of business to learn is that just because you can make *one* type of business prosper does not mean you will automatically do the same with others.

I guess if there is a second rule, it is to be ever ready to cut and run. I have always had a deep, abiding hatred of business losses and—call it chicken if you will—as soon as a company started losing a substantial amount of money, I started cutting every expense I could. It's simple. You start at the top of your profit-and-loss statement, and you cut down or out every possibly expendable expense account. Usually it leaves you with a smaller operation—but upon regrouping, still a fighting, lean one capable of making it again. If you know it is not, sell it or close it down before it drags you down with it.

While building companies, one must be wary of overextending either financial or personnel resources. Many a good group of companies has fallen on the rocks because the owner, too eager (or greedy?) to build, got careless along the way. Anything worthwhile accomplishing in this world requires a sound, strong base, and the growth of companies is no exception. It is worth repeating:

> And look before you ere you leap;
> For as you sow, ye are like to reap.

Returning to your question, whether we would not be better off operating only one company and putting all our resources into its growth, I would consider it only if that company required all my available time for the management of its growth. If it did not, then I would have time to pursue other business endeavors—which, I must admit, greatly relieves some of the boredom and humdrum of day-to-day business routines. Of course, careful financial planning would also be a requisite for guarding against any overextension of our resources.

Business is so very fragile. Considering that companies the size of such giants as those in the auto industry sometimes almost go under, one has to marvel at the audacity of us small guys trying to make a buck out there. But no business, big or small, lasts forever. The laws of supply and demand, ever fluctuating virtually beyond anyone's prediction or control, often require almost psychic powers of the business executives trying to keep pace with them. Few of us are endowed with psychic powers.

Diversification, to me, does not mean or entail straying from your base industry. Rather, it means *adding* to your main product lines by purchasing other companies or a major supplier. For us to plunge into computers, picture frames, furniture, auto accessories, retail outlets, or the like would be improvident and foolhardy, since our best expertise lies within none of these areas. We would end up in the graveyard.

I have adhered to another important principle when diversifying—that of buying not companies, but rather good people who know how to run them. There is no more naked feeling than knowing that management virtually not worth a hoot is trying to run one of your companies. In one company, I once went through three general managers in three years, trying to make it work. Drove myself crazy—probably over the disappointment of my people selections—and almost sold the blasted company in frustration. My last attempt (wish it had been my first) was to take a long shot on a long-term company employee under whom everyone swore they would not work. I let him have a go at it. It worked. With an added bonus: our employee turnover actually dropped to 3 percent.

Andrew Carnegie wrote the often proved truism, "Three generations from shirt-sleeves to shirt-sleeves." I am just trying to steer clear of having to return to shirt-sleeves in *one* generation. And once I am through with the business, you are welcome to try *your* hand at proving Mr. Carnegie wrong. Until then I'll chart the course and you master the ship.

Affectionately,

Captain Ward

The Value of Reading

$\mathcal{D}$ear Son:

You will recall that somewhere in your flying experience you ran across the expression, "Learn from others' mistakes; you won't have time to make them all by yourself." The same applies to books, in a way. If people have written of experiences that upon being read might be of benefit to you—why not give yourself this available edge on life and read what they have to say about handling various situations?

There is not much new under the sun except for such scientific breakthroughs, of course, as the dropping of atomic bombs, walking on the moon, and the development of computers. But most business decisions have been made over and over again and most have been described in writing in some book or other. If you take the time and patience to read, you will have a major headstart on most other fellows your age who do not.

The best book I can think of to illustrate my point to you that not much is new under the sun—and how repetitive mankind's lifetimes are—is *Bartlett's Quotations*. This book begins with reflections on life as far back as in the Bible and comes forward through the ages to the present day. In it you will discover that Homer said in about 700 B.C., "For rarely are sons similar to their fathers: most are worse, and a few are better than their fathers." Confucius said in 500 B.C., "Have no friends not equal to yourself." Aesop said in 550 B.C., "Be content with your lot; one cannot be first in everything." St. Jerome said in 400 A.D., "It is worse still to be ignorant of your ignorance." *Bartlett's* continues in like manner to the end, infusing its reader with the thoughts and views of countless people in countless generations—all living and breathing, experiencing life at one time or another just as you and I are now. I believe that familiarizing ourselves with these thinkers' attitudes, opinions, and problems often makes *our* problems appear pale by comparison—or at least a lot easier to solve because of their experienced observations.

I feel that at my stage of the game, simply because of my reading, I have already lived the equivalent of about ten lifetimes of experience. Not that that gives me any feeling of superiority. It doesn't. But it sure does make me feel I am getting the most out of my time here on earth. And I feel sorry for anyone born into any manner of tight, little community who never gets the opportunity of seeing beyond it—physically, or mentally through books—whether of choice or no choice. How little they learn of life. How much they miss of life!

Some people read a lot, but mostly fiction. They say that it relaxes them. Many feel reading nonfiction is *work.* Funny, I never feel anything but *relaxed* when reading nonfiction. Plus, with so many things in this universe to learn about, so many truths far more fascinating than fiction to read about, I almost feel it a waste of time reading somebody's *daydreams.*

John Locke said in 1670, "No man's knowledge here can go beyond his experience." I would agree with that

—but one's own experience can be broadened vastly by reading about others' experiences. According to the grapevine, Harry Truman, as vice president of the United States, was considered very poorly qualified for the position of president. Still, despite his little experience, old Harry became a very strong president. My theory about his success is that it was largely due to the fact that, at age fourteen, he had read every book in the small local library in Independence, Missouri. His reading gave him the required insight into world problems that his position demanded but that his experience had not yet caught up with.

History is a series of stories I find most stimulating, rewarding, and enjoyable—about the courage of men flying aircraft in World War I, about the thinking of Confucius on man and society, about the trials of Richard the Lion-Hearted in building England. Fascinating. So many heroic deeds gloriously accomplished, so many tribulations faced and overcome, so many major problems solved by so many people. They make a lot of our meager efforts look puny by comparison. However, whatever length our journey in life might be, it must still begin with but one single step—and each book is another step in the right direction.

To be able to see in one's mind another's journey or achievement, another's rationale of the solution to a problem is as close as one can get to actual experience. Books do that. They open our minds to wondering and thinking about why we are here, to trying to do the best we can, and to the realization that anything less on our part is to throw away a large portion of the time each of us has been allotted on this earth.

Being different from others is one of the requisites of success—yet so few people will dare it. Most of the major

117

decisions I have made were usually bucked by my friends. In all good conscience, they kept warning me how risky what I was attempting to do was, how the odds were all against me or how foolhardy I was being. Upon attaining my degree as a cpa, when I turned aside jobs in large corporations in favor of employment with a very small company, I was ridiculed by my contemporaries. Our business today is a direct result of that decision. Learning to fly at forty was considered *iffy* business by many because I had a young family. That decision resulted in years of enjoyment for our whole family. And in Yul Brynner's immortal words from *The King and I,* "Et cetera, et cetera, et cetera."

To improve your business skills by reading is simply to read about *people.* History is about people. And scores of current, widely read books on such topics as stress, investing money, dieting, exercise, flying safety, and innumerable others are all about people and what they think or what they have done. Read about people in a wide spectrum if you want your skills in business to improve immeasurably.

As to which books to read about particular business subjects, call on some of the former professors of your business courses. They are usually very up to date on who wrote what or where the best treatise on a certain subject can be found. Use them as your advisers. (I always found them eager to help—and the price was right.)

You will recall that I built a bookshelf in your room when you were nineteen. On it I placed ten books I felt would be of immense value to you in business and in your personal life. They were the following:

1. *Bartlett's Familiar Quotations*
        —John Bartlett

2. *My Life in Advertising*
   —Claude Hopkins, 1927

3. *The Nature of a Family Business*
   —Léon Danco, 1981

4. *The Doctor and the Soul*
   —Viktor E. Frankl, M.D., 1955

5. *Our Oriental Heritage*
   —Will Durant, 1935

6. *Think and Grow Rich*
   —Napoleon Hill, 1937

7. *The Rising Sun*
   —John Toland, 1970

8. One book of the *Encyclopaedia Britannica*

9. *The History of the Decline and Fall of the Roman Empire*
   —Edward Gibbon, 1788

10. *Ralph Waldo Emerson: Representative Selections*
   —Frederic I. Carpenter, 1934

Now I would like to leave you with the words of St. Thomas Aquinas in 1250: "Beware of the man of one book." Need I say more?

Sincerely,

Bookworm

P.S.

Following is a copy of my favorite book. Since it is but a few pages long, most people would not call it a book. I do, because its message is so important.

———

The following story was written in a single hour in 1899. Notwithstanding the casualness that its author, Elbert Hubbard, displayed in its creation, the message that it contained was so vital and basic that as early as 1913, forty million copies of the original work had been printed. During the Russo-Japanese War, every Russian soldier going to the front carried a copy of "A Message to Garcia." The Japanese, impressed by the multitude of copies they confiscated from their Russian prisoners, concluded that a translation should be immediately carried out and later, upon orders of the Mikado, a copy was given to every man in the employ of the government, both soldier and civilian. It has been translated into Russian, German, French, Spanish, Turkish, Hindustani, Japanese, and Chinese. In all probability, numerous other translations also exist. Although the moral message was obviously current at the time of its writing, it appears even more incisive today.

A MESSAGE TO GARCIA

In all this Cuban business there is one man stands out on the horizon of my memory like Mars at perihelion.

When war broke out between Spain and the United States, it was very necessary to communicate quickly with the leader of the Insurgents. Garcia was somewhere in the mountain fastnesses of Cuba—no one knew where. No mail or telegraph message could reach him. The President must secure his co-operation, and quickly.

What to do!

Someone said to the President, "There is a fellow by the name of Rowan will find Garcia for you, if anybody can."

Rowan was sent for and given a letter to be delivered to Garcia. How the "fellow by the name of Rowan" took the letter, sealed it up in an oilskin pouch, strapped it over his heart, in four days landed by night off the coast of Cuba from an open boat, disappeared into the jungle, and in three weeks came out on the other side of the Island, having traversed a hostile country on foot, and delivered his letter to Garcia—are things I have no special desire now to tell in detail. The point that I wish to make is this: McKinley gave Rowan a letter to be delivered to Garcia; Rowan took the letter and did not ask, "Where is he at?"

By the Eternal! there is a man whose form should be cast in deathless bronze and the statue placed in every college of the land. It is not book-learning young men need, nor instruction about this and that, but a stiffening of the vertebrae which will cause them to be loyal to a trust, to act promptly, concentrate their energies: do the thing—"Carry a message to Garcia."

General Garcia is dead now, but there are other Garcias. No man who has endeavored to carry out an enterprise where many hands are needed, but has been well-nigh appalled by the imbecility of the average man —the inability or unwillingness to concentrate on a thing and do it.

Slipshod assistance, foolish inattention, dowdy indifference, and half-hearted work seem the rule; and no man succeeds, unless by hook or crook or threat he forces or bribes other men to assist him; or mayhap, God in His goodness performs a miracle, and sends him an Angel of Light for an assistant.

You, reader, put this matter to a test. You are sitting now in your office—six clerks are within call. Summon any one and make this request: "Please look in the encyclopedia and make a brief memorandum for me concerning the life of Correggio."

Will the clerk quietly say, "Yes, sir," and go do the task?

On your life he will not. He will look at you out of a fishy eye and ask one or more of the following questions:

Who was he?

Which encyclopedia?

Where is the encyclopedia?

Don't you mean Bismarck?

What's the matter with Charlie doing it?

Is he dead?

Is there any hurry?

Sha'n't I bring you the book and let you look it up yourself?

What do you want to know for?

And I will lay you ten to one that after you have answered the questions, and explained how to find the information, and why you want it, the clerk will go off and get one of the other clerks to help him try to find Garcia —and then come back and tell you there is no such man. Of course I may lose my bet, but according to the Law of Average I will not.

Now, if you are wise, you will not bother to explain to your "assistant" that Correggio is indexed under the C's, not in the K's, but you will smile very sweetly and say, "Never mind," and then look it up yourself. And this incapacity for independent action, this moral stupidity, this infirmity of the will, this unwillingness to cheerfully catch hold and lift—these are the things that put pure Socialism so far into the future. If men will not act for themselves, what will they do when the benefit of their effort is for all?

A first mate with knotted club seems necessary; and the dread of getting "the bounce" Saturday night holds many a worker to his place. Advertise for a stenographer, and nine out of ten who apply can neither spell nor punctuate—and do not think it necessary to.

Can such a one write a letter to Garcia?

"You see that bookkeeper," said the foreman to me in a large factory.

"Yes, what about him?"

"Well, he's a fine accountant, but if I'd send him uptown on an errand, he might accomplish the errand all right, and on the other hand, might stop at four saloons on the way, and when he got to Main Street would forget what he had been sent for."

Can such a man be entrusted to carry a message to Garcia?

We have recently been hearing much maudlin sympathy expressed for the "downtrodden denizens of the sweat-shop" and the "homeless wanderer searching for honest employment," and with it all often go many hard words for the men in power.

Nothing is said about the employer who grows old before his time in a vain attempt to get frowsy ne'er-do-wells to do intelligent work; and his long, patient striving after "help" that does nothing but loaf when his back is turned. In every store and factory there is a constant weeding-out process going on. The employer is constantly sending away "help" that have shown their incapacity to further the interests of the business, and others are being taken on.

No matter how good times are, this sorting continues: only, if times are hard and work is scarce, the sorting is done finer—but out and forever out the incompetent and unworthy go. It is the survival of the fittest. Self-interest prompts every employer to keep the best—those who can carry a message to Garcia.

I know one man of really brilliant parts who has not the ability to manage a business of his own, and yet who is absolutely worthless to anyone else, because he carries with him constantly the insane suspicion that his employer is oppressing, or intending to oppress him. He can not give orders, and he will not receive them. Should a message be given him to take to Garcia, his answer would probably be, "Take it yourself!"

Tonight this man walks the streets looking for work, the wind whistling through his threadbare coat. No one who knows him dare employ him, for he is a regular firebrand of discontent. He is impervious to reason, and the only thing that can impress him is the toe of a thick-soled Number Nine boot.

Of course I know that one so morally deformed is no less to be pitied than a physical cripple; but in our pitying let us drop a tear, too, for the men who are striving to carry on a great enterprise, whose working hours are not limited by the whistle, and whose hair is fast turning white through the struggle to hold in line dowdy indifference, slipshod imbecility, and the heartless ingratitude which, but for their enterprise, would be both hungry and homeless.

Have I put the matter too strongly? Possibly I have; but when all the world has gone a-slumming I wish to speak a word of sympathy for the man who succeeds— the man who, against great odds, has directed the efforts of others, and having succeeded, finds there's nothing in it: nothing but bare board and clothes. I have carried a dinner-pail and worked for day's wages, and I have also been an employer of labor, and I know there is something to be said on both sides. There is no excellence, per se, in poverty; rags are no recommendation; and all employers are not rapacious and high-handed, any more than all poor men are virtuous. My heart goes out to the man who does his work when the "boss" is away, as well as when he is at home. And the man who, when given a letter for Garcia, quietly takes the missive, without asking any idiotic questions, and with no lurking intention of chucking it into the nearest sewer, or of doing aught else but deliver it, never gets "laid off," nor has to go on a strike for higher wages. Civilization is one long, anxious search for just such individuals. Anything such a man asks shall be granted. He is wanted in every city, town and village—in every office, shop, store and factory. The world cries out for such: he is needed and needed badly —the man who can "Carry a Message to Garcia."

Teamwork

ear Son:

It was interesting to see you sweat a little today over the new policy in motion to modernize our manufacturing company's capabilities. I say it was "interesting" because you *admitted you were stuck* concerning the best route to follow. I guess all that schooling and your few years in the real world are beginning to show some promise— for only when you openly admit to a problem, admit it has you scratching your head, are you truly joining the elite group of those who are becoming successful.

A man who is able to admit to a problem already has one of the two most important characteristics of being a good man. The other main trait—of which I have not seen too many signs from you as yet—is being able to admit to *failure.* No doubt your reply to that is, "Well, you will when I do!" I hope I live long enough to see it, because then there will not be too much else left for me to pass on to you.

I do not know how many days or weeks of your valuable time (and my more valuable money) you have already spent on this problem before telling me about it —but whatever amount of time it was, over one day was too long. The obvious recourse, employing a much overworked but greatly underplayed word, was *teamwork.*

Before bringing in equipment that will reduce a considerable portion of the work now being done by human hands, one must first, of course, establish if there is enough money for it. Well, with your certified public accountant's training and some good business lessons of the past, you have convinced our bankers they should lend us the money if you present them with a sensible program.

In accordance with the principle of inflation, our labor costs per unit of output will continue increasing, year after year, for the foreseeable future. A piece of equipment has a fixed cost and, once paid for, becomes free labor—assuming, of course, we are still in business. More than one company executive carried away with the idea of progress has overextended himself purchasing equipment—with a business downturn shortly thereafter, and the bankruptcy courts after that. (I know this is the 326th time I have told you that, but remind me of it, please, only when I hit the 1000th time.)

Now comes the segment in the preparation of your program that has you stumped, mainly because you have not as yet had enough experience in this department. For which areas do we buy new, modern equipment? Your quandary is not surprising since you have overlooked one of your best methods of solving this particular problem. The one called *teamwork.*

In your analysis of the areas in which most hand labor is employed, start with your cost accountant's assistance. Compare your top machine-equipped line costs with those that are semiautomatic, and so forth. But wait, wouldn't the plant manager also be a logical person with whom to discuss this area? He can tell you where auto-mation would work best and for which volume level of products. The floor supervisors, even closer than he to actual production, will probably have further input to offer, perhaps of even greater validity. Might be interesting to ask our quality-control people which areas in their opinion are causing the most problems. Highly significant information to your analysis. And if you think you have now covered everything, stop and look about you for a minute. How about the mechanics, who can tell you and me more than anyone else about our equipment, its condition, and which company in their experienced opinion makes the best equipment?

This is what I call effective management—utilizing your personnel's experience and brainpower, keeping your people posted, asking their opinions and advice— in short, *teamwork*. Nothing makes a person's chest stick out further than being asked his opinion on a subject he knows is of special importance to the asker. It makes one feel his judgment is valued. Never miss an opportunity to sincerely display how much you value your employees. They are our lifeblood!

Compiling the data for this type of report requires tact, discernment, and discretion. Oh, does it require all three!—and unless you carefully bear it in mind, you could find yourself with one unholy mess on your hands, your people jumping to all sorts of conjectures and conclusions. You are trying to eliminate their jobs! You are reducing the number of people under them! You are trying to cut corners! The company must be in trouble. . . . Clear it all up at the very start—at the very beginning of all your meetings.

As I see it, although the reduction of hand labor will lower the new hirings we presently average within our growth pattern, and although some jobs will have to be

realigned, no one will lose his or her job. As a matter of fact, most of our employees should soon be looking for *bigger* paychecks—even allowing for inflation—for the more efficient we become, the more we should be able to go after and get some of our competition's business for the plant.

As the head man, you will need to hold a firm hand on the tiller should differences of opinion or arguments erupt among your team. If you accept a mechanic's recommendation over that of his supervisor's, be sure to diplomatically explain your decision to the supervisor. One tactful approach is to concede that while time might very well prove him right, you would rather he did not oppose your decision at this juncture. (If he still does, you might want to add that parting might *not* be such sweet sorrow.)

Now comes the exciting part: spending the money. Here is where you either make or break your case, so do your homework very carefully or we could be asking for more troubles than a grouse has feathers. From the equipment companies, find and study the available models under consideration. Select them, of course, in accordance with the volume sizes we want; no use buying a capper with a 300-per-minute capacity if that of our filler and labeler is only 100 per minute. We need a balanced line. And bear in mind, before we can package 25,000 units a shift on a line, we must first be able to manufacture that quantity. *Keep it a nice straight line of Chevrolets. No Lincolns, please.*

Before purchasing any piece of new equipment, make certain you observe the unit in actual use. Find someone who owns it, ask to see it, and take a mechanic and the plant manager along with you to ask pertinent questions about its operation. Nothing is more illuminating than observing how an owner uses the machine and how satisfied he is with it. If the equipment does not perform as he was told it would, no doubt he will be quick to tell you so. No one likes to be taken. If he has been, he will probably be eager to tell you about it, to spare your making the same mistake.

Finally, make certain you investigate such particulars as changeover time and the availability of parts and servicing by the dealer. Then you should be ready to make your decision *in conference* with the rest of your team. It would not be fair to "pick their brains" through the whole game and then exclude them from the victory celebration.

Upon delivery of the new equipment, after setup and shakeout, you will be able to judge how good a decision your team made. Let them in on the "score," so to speak. If you collectively picked out a good piece, tell them— so they can cheer along with me. If you goofed, tell them —so if they overhear me calling you a blockhead, they will understand why. In my estimation, the blame would indeed all fall on *your* shoulders, but if my measurements of these people are correct, your team would feel a lot worse about it than you—and without a solitary direct word from me, they would make damn sure the next purchase was a real humdinger. ("Couldn't have the old man thinking we're a bunch of idiots! Only the best from us can be good enough!")

Teamwork pulls many, *many* years of experience and effort together, yet it is one of the least used tools of business. Remember when you were a quarterback? No matter how good *you* were during any one game, your team's winning seasons only occurred when the morale of the *entire* team was high and when the greatest effort was exerted by each and every player. Same thing here, in the real world.

However, after all has been said and done, I know—and I want you to remember—it really *is* impossible to please all the world *and* your father, all the time.

Signed,

Mr. Perfection Himself

On Happiness

$\mathscr{D}$ear Son:

During our recent fishing trip together, you posed some philosophical queries: "How does one attain 'real' happiness in life?" "What makes a person a 'man'?" "Why are some people the kind you always feel pleased and happy to be with, while others make five minutes in their presence feel more like a week?"

The ten-pound pike on your line interrupted our train of conversation, but I would very much like to continue it now. The questions you ask are ones I have spent a considerable part of my time on earth trying to answer for myself. People have many different theories on all three topics. About your first query, the writings of Viktor E. Frankl, an Austrian psychiatrist who survived the Nazi concentration camps in World War II, have been among the most informative of my readings and have perhaps influenced my own thinking on the subject most. He developed new theories on happiness. Freud felt life's happiness is achieved through pleasure. Adler felt it is gained through the pursuit of power. Well, compared with Dr. Frankl's sentiments, I am afraid the latter two gentlemen missed the boat completely as far as I am concerned. We will go into this further later on.

What makes a man a man? Well, I would think the first essential is the realization that everyone owns a *spirit* —a unique, one and one only, individual spirit created *by* oneself *unto* oneself. Only when you comprehend that fact, and that you are in charge of it, and what power it puts at your disposal can you really begin to *do your own thing.* Only then will you not always be waiting for others, walking with others, looking to others for help. You will be looking primarily to *yourself.* Because it can only be created by you, your spirit is a combination of human cells uniquely your own and unlike any other in any other soul. Hence, all other souls have but limited bearing on the development of this aspect of your being. Francis Bacon wrote, "Chiefly the mold of a man's fortune is in his own hands." So, too, is the molding of a man's spirit.

Freedom plays the basic, fundamental role in the development of one's spirit, yet few people pause to realize it. Few are consciously aware of the freedom each of us exercises every time we accept or reject an instinct. The very core of strength within every human being is the freedom to choose how one wants to respond to life's challenges. Given a difficult job to do, you can decide whether you will complain about it and your lot in life, or whether you will say to yourself, "This is a difficult, distasteful job, but I will do it and do it well." If you choose to accept the latter attitude, it will make your job easier to do and, more importantly, it will provide a sense of accomplishment at the end. Discovering and fully exercising your freedom to choose your attitudes toward the challenges of life will vastly affect your rate of success with happiness in life.

Upon developing your spirit and exercising your freedom of choice of attitude, *responsibilities* of life become easier to acknowledge, accept, and fulfill. It stands to reason. Responsibility is, in Frankl's words, "the foundation of human existence." It is an observation of mine that the people who accept responsibility are the people who are making the most of their lives. Another observation is that many people have an inherent fear of accepting responsibility much akin to the fear of failure. I wish I could remind each such person individually that to have tried and failed is no disgrace; not to have tried is disaster. Accepting responsibility is accepting challenge; accepting challenges throws open the doors through which glorious achievements enter our lives.

Reading about the great people who have lived and live now on this earth is reading about great individual spirits: none trampled by their fellow men, all steering through life with compasses in their hearts constantly set at freedom of choice and attitude and the acceptance of individual responsibility. Never do I read about the lives of any of these great persons, and the failures and disappointments they overcame while scaling to their great heights of success, without becoming awed by their forbearance, courage, and tenacity. "It is a rough road that leads to heights of greatness," said Seneca back in 50 A.D. That same road is no smoother today.

Making key decisions is the password, for on *that* balance point rests how your life will fare. At each fork in your road, you will have to decide which direction you want to follow—but first you have to decide to *walk* the road.

There are many, many people today—especially among the young—who are unhappy and find little meaning to their lives. Perhaps a lack of *goals* is largely responsible. Without goals, there are no achievements or accomplishments bringing them happiness. For some reason, they fail to tap the potential power of their abilities—and for that same reason, they will undoubtedly one day look in a mirror and say, in Friedrich Hebbel's words:

> The man I am, greets mournfully
> the man I might have been.

People say our relatively high standard of living, to a great degree, can be blamed for creating laziness and discontent. Well, there is nothing new about that. Greek, Roman, and other cultures have experienced unrest and unhappiness among their youth, and among many of their adults as well. No, it is not our standard of living that is chiefly at fault; it is the failure to develop spirit, failure to recognize that one is unto himself, failure to utilize freedom of choice and attitude in our decision making, failure to accept responsibility. Only when all these enter one's life is there meaning and purpose to one's existence.

Seems to me that rather than honorably *fighting* to survive anymore, a lot of people have taken to *running*—running to the security of government welfare or the church or friends, or to assorted other sociological crutches, including, of course, drugs and alcohol. Never having experienced success and failure in sufficient quantities to acquire it, they have no moral reserve for help over the rough spots. These sad souls do not know that the only real antidote against difficulties can come from within, from that freedom of choice each of us possesses in deciding which attitudes we will adopt—positive or negative—against the knocks of life. Such people hide, reading fiction or watching fictional television heroes and heroines portraying fictional accomplishments in life—ever content to let someone else, even make-believe characters—do the things in life they would *like* to do, but never try. Sad. My remedy? Pick up some *non*fiction, learn what *real* human beings have accomplished or are accomplishing in life, and say to yourself, "Hey! Why not me?"

Dr. Frankl, in his book *The Doctor and the Soul*, says all this and more far better than I. His definition of happiness is *achievement*, and when you stop to consider it, might he not be absolutely right? It is pretty hard to just sit yourself down and *tell* yourself you are going to be happy—except, of course, about your good health or fine family. Happiness is not something you can create out of nothing or from material objects—even those basics of life surrounding you. I agree with Dr. Frankl that our finest moments of true happiness occur upon the achievement of some goal we have set for ourselves. It might be as simple as cleaning up the backyard or as outstanding as being elected by your fellow human beings to some station in life. Happiness can be helping someone—a friend or, better still, someone you don't know. It is also earning successful marks in school, learning how to drive a car, fly an airplane, ride a bike. Happiness is *doing*.

Your grandfather was a happy man in life reaching goals most people would not call big successes. But for him they were the *great* goals! The peace and contentment he felt within after a hard day's work. And I can tell you there were a good many of those. His life was one of continual hard work at one thing or another. On his eightieth birthday, when I asked him how he was doing, he replied he had no quarrels with life as long as he had something to do when he woke up every morning. (That goal!) At eighty-five, when he no longer had *the somethings to look forward to* daily, his health deteriorated rapidly.

Putting meaning into our lives is putting quality into our life spans. A single moment, a single task can put a good measure or all of it there. Acceptance of the good days and the bad with equal resolve to do our best in both can put it there. Facing whatever the future holds with courage and dignity can put it there.

Happiness accompanies achievement. Achievement is the product of freely made choices and attitudes, accepted and fulfilled responsibilities, and strong, indomitable spirits ever willing to *try*.

The value of life lies not in the length of days, but in the use we make of them: a man may live long, yet get little from life. Whether you find satisfaction [happiness] in life depends not on your tale of years, but on your will.

So said Montaigne about 400 years ago.
Happily,

Your Fellow Road Walker

On Firing People

$\mathcal{D}$ear Son:

Your concern and discomfort over having to terminate the services of our office manager is a sensitivity I like to see in a person. It means you care about your fellow human beings, means you are aware what upset and despair the carrying out of such a duty might wreak upon the lives of others. I like your heart.

If I may act as the devil's advocate, however, you must never lose sight of the fact that the success of your business hinges on the quality and quantity of work performed by your employees collectively and individually. If an employee is simply not suited for his job, he is of negative value to the company—negative as opposed to the value of a person with the right qualifications for the work. Unfortunately, the person of negative value to a company—because he cannot help but sense that reality, usually finds himself in the same boat on a personal level. Understandably so. It is pretty difficult to leave all your woes at the office when you are swimming against a tide trying to push you out to sea eight hours out of every day.

Some executive employees experience difficulty with

their jobs simply because they have bitten off more than they can chew. They want the higher pay and the title of the position but in one way or another are underqualified to handle it. Such an executive's business life becomes one of constant struggle and turmoil—and ours one of declining faith and trust in his efforts.

Then there is the other end of the spectrum—the person who is overqualified for his position and bored to death with it all. He faces each day much as does the sailor who has become becalmed: "loves the area but cannot stand the lack of action." He too becomes of negative value to his company, for with no enthusiasm being brought to his desk daily, neither he nor the company can possibly benefit and sooner or later it becomes imperative for the two to part company.

Somewhere in this scenario you also sometimes find a person whose personality causes dissension and morale problems among the employees around him. I have seen instances of people with terrific potential of becoming eminently valuable to our company—who loved their jobs—but could just not fit in with their co-workers. Clearly as the writing on a wall, one could detect the growing unease among the other workers as they lost more and more of their interest and liking for their duties. Any person causing this kind of dissension *must* go—before his attitude drives your *valuable* employees out the door.

In our case at hand, you have a person with whom, in my opinion, it is most difficult to work whether one happens to be his subordinate *or* his boss. Although his work is competent enough and acceptable, his personality and attitude are absolutely not. Too often does he distinctly indicate that certain of our functions are beneath his dignity to perform. It is time they were all removed from beneath his control. Many employers allow such situations to continue indefinitely, rationalizing that there are enough good days left among the bad to justify employment. I call that procrastination. Releasing a person from his duties is never a pleasant task. Nevertheless it is one that must be faced when it is warranted and no amount of procrastination will ever make it easier.

I have had to terminate a number of people in my time—as you will have to do, probably more frequently, in your time—and I have never left one of these sessions without wondering, "Did I do the right thing?" Asking myself the same question a month or two later, however, there was not a doubt in my mind I had not only done the right thing, but that I should have done it a lot sooner!

Prior to the time you terminate an employee, devote some thought to the person's abilities and strengths that might be far better utilized elsewhere. Has a skill of his been underused at our place of business? Is he trying to cope with a job here for which he is underskilled (our mistake, not his)? If it is a personality problem for us, might that very personality be an asset somewhere else? Whatever the case, it is important to let the person down as easily as possible. This way you both win. *You* have not made an enemy, and *he* should be able to relocate without going through too much agony. It is the least one can do to help his fellow man.

Toward this same end, be as light as possible in your criticism when you are asked the inevitable "why?" You need not lie, for that would only demean *both* parties. Instead, quietly explain in very few words why you have reached your decision and why the other person will be better off for it in the long run. "I'm sorry, it's a problem of personalities." "I'm sorry, your talents don't match the job." "I'm sorry, but I know you will be happier elsewhere."

On each such occasion, I try to move quickly to the subject of a recommendation and discussion about relocating. There is not a man or woman who has ever worked for me for whom I did not, or could not, provide a letter of recommendation (although I am sure there are many in the world for whom one could not). By arming the person you have just let go with a letter of recommendation and your assistance in relocating him, you will very much be helping him overcome his worst and foremost fear: "Where will I get another job?" This kind of help is usually gratefully accepted and well appreciated for its value. It is common knowledge that most prospective employers today do check a person's references prior to hiring him. Try to make sure your person leaves your office not wondering *how* he or she is going to get a job, but only *when.*

The *when* will still be accompanied by concern and anguish over finances, of course, before a new job is secured. Our laws are quite fair with respect to senior executives in these situations, stipulating that a portion of salary must be continued while the person seeks new employment, the amount contingent on the length of time the person has spent in the company's employ. I personally feel every employer owes an employee this kind of protection, especially in the case of long-term employees.

Occasionally, a sticky situation arises during an employee's termination due to dissatisfaction with your proffered terms of severance pay. Sometimes—even though you might not feel the person is worth the money

—an extra month or two of salary can avoid the lawyers, the courts, and most of all, the vindictiveness of some disgruntled ex-employees.

Unavoidably, any employee who is terminated must feel a measure of failure, a measure of fear, loss of pride, anguish, and turmoil. As a cocitizen of this universe, it is your duty to minimize these feelings as much as you can, both personally and financially. If you do, then no matter how difficult, trying, unpleasant, or messy any such occasion might turn out to be, rest assured at least *one* of you will be walking away with his head held high. *You.*

Let it be indelibly stamped on your mind and your heart that only the most careful and keenest selection of employees at the outset will reduce these less than happy occasions in business. But even that will not eliminate them all; the comings and goings of people within business communities has been in existence forever and will be forevermore.

There are pleasurable jobs in business as well as some that are not so pleasurable; both kinds are integrally involved in the running of any forward-moving operation. You cannot duck the tough ones and expect to enjoy only the appealing ones. So get on with this tough one. With *heart.*

Yours truly,

The Personnel Manager

Friendship

$\mathcal{D}$ear Son:

What has friendship to do with business? Well, in some ways, a lot; in other ways, less than zero if it is but a veil cloaking someone's devious method of "getting something" through someone else. In the business world, you meet many people—virtually a cross section of society—with whom you associate: plant employees, buyers, suppliers, customers, government officials, all of whom supplement those you meet outside business: neighbors, church and club members, store clerks, garage mechanics, and, in our case, other pilots and fishermen. That's a lot of people. Not all of them become your friends in a close way, but all do, to some measure, contribute to your happiness of association here on earth.

Samuel Johnson once said, "I look upon every day to be lost, in which I do not make a new acquaintance." Good thought. For from where else can friendships spring? One meets someone new, pleasantries are exchanged, conversation leads to rapport, and a friendship often begins with a "Let's have lunch sometime" as the friendly catalyst. Incidentally, never extend that invitation unless you mean it, for lack of follow-through is often interpreted as shallow thinking.

From such chance meetings in life sprout the very basic genes of friendship, with human nature automatically letting you know whose company you prefer on your private Friendship Trail. Nothing is as fruitless or as frustrating as trying to cultivate a friendship with someone who feels no chemistry between himself and you. Only thing worse is you feeling no chemistry while someone else is fervently attempting to befriend you. But be gentle on such occasions. If the pursuit of friendship is genuine, it means someone has found something about you he admires, so don't blame him unduly for seeking a closer relationship with you.

Of embryos of acquaintances are born some of the world's strongest friendships. Usually the greatest of these magnificent human bonds exists in the friendship between a man and his wife. Son, hopefully, your second will be the friendship you share with your children; after that, with your father and mother, and then your in-laws. I say *hopefully*, because one of life's frequently repeated tragedies is the abandonment of friendship between those whom blood ties or marriage ceremonies have bound together. These closest and most precious of friendships require constant care and kindling. So, too, do the friendships between you and mankind outside your family; they as well need to be nurtured to remain intact.

A characteristic habit of strong people is to have (as in 500 B.C. Confucius said) "no friends not equal to yourself." To me, his counsel suggests we can aid ourselves in life by befriending only people of equal or greater standards as compared to our own; people capable of influencing us only toward becoming better, never less than what we are. Makes good sense to me. And I believe it goes even further.

Being liked by someone you respect and admire cannot help but bolster your confidence for it signifies you in turn are being respected, admired, sought out for conversation or companionship. One of the nicest feelings or compliments is being invited to attend something with a person or couple you admire—especially if it is for a special occasion or an intimate get-together.

You have heard me expounding many times on how little of our brain power we all use in life and how much of our potential brain power lies fallow. There is nothing like some good, stimulating conversation with a friend of stature to stoke up and expand that brain power—nothing like it to get more out of life or to put more into it.

Sir William Osler has a few words for you: "In the life of a young man the most essential thing for happiness is the gift of friendship." Truer words were never spoken. For what more could you ask than comradeship during the peaks and valleys of life? To whom else but a close, valuable *friend* can you brag about your successes and whine about your failures or losses?

What is a "good friend"? How is he best described? Well, it has been my observation that although many will *cry* with you, few can sincerely *rejoice* with you. Therefore, in my opinion, a good friend is one who can enjoy your successes without envy; one who can say, "That was wonderful! You can do it again, even *better* if you want!"— and mean it. Nothing taxes a friendship more than the prosperity of one and not the other. Even the closest of friendships (and marriages) often cannot withstand such strain and collapse. Small wonder many minor friendships go down the drain for the same reason.

A person of good character and sound moral fiber, of

145

honor and humor, courage and conviction is a friend to be sought, coddled, and treasured—for there are few. Too often do we hear, "If you can count your good friends on more than one hand, consider yourself blessed." And even then I would add, "Even if you have lost two fingers of that hand to the electric saw."

What makes a friendship last? Well, I don't know all the answers, but one of my observations is that most good friends usually have similar tastes. They generally like and dislike many of the same things. There also usually seems to exist a parallelism of personality traits —especially in the fundamental values of life such as honesty, sincerity, loyalty, and dependability. More often than not, birds of a feather *do* fly together. I don't think it matters a hoot whether one prefers jazz or hockey to another's Mozart or ballet. Much other matters *far* more: confiding, relying, sharing, giving, getting, enjoying; a sympathetic ear always there; criticism when it can help; praise—even if only because it *would* help. With not many people on this earth will you find this much in common. When you find one, hang on to him, for a good friend found is a rare treasure.

Initiating or maintaining a good friendship involves reaching out, time, thoughtfulness and care, a phone call at least once a month, a lunch every two months or so. Do not allow too much water to pass under the bridge between contacts. Good friendships need tending. Just as a farmer's rail fence gets checked and repaired regularly to prevent his cattle from wandering away, so too must the bonds of friendship be checked and any snags repaired to avert a good friend—through neglect—from wandering off.

Making new friends as we go through life is essential. He who does not will soon find solitude his bosom companion more often than he might wish. There are a hell of a lot of witty, intelligent, highly interesting people in this world. You cannot meet them all, but you will—I dearly hope—take the time to try and meet many. Without doubt, friendship is the spice of life. I never fail to enjoy conversing with a new friend and listening to his points of view on life. Whether I agree with him or not does not matter. If I respect my new friend, I will respect his views—and expect the same from him in return. Lively debate will sharpen our senses, tap our brain powers and, all in all, enhance and enliven our lives.

I wish I had met Samuel Johnson, who lived in the eighteenth century, but unfortunately, since he has long been dead, I have had to carry on my friendship with him through his written thoughts. He had a brilliant outlook on life and mankind—or perhaps better expressed, he possessed brilliant *insight.* His writings attest to it and to the fact that he was a man of great common sense.

He lived to be seventy-five years of age—far and away beyond the average life expectancy of those days, and I am convinced his clearheaded attitude toward life and mankind had a lot to do with it. I am equally convinced it made his time on this earth enjoyable—probably a good deal more enjoyable than most of us experience. Two years before his death he wrote:

To let friendship die away by negligence and silence, is certainly not wise. It is voluntarily to throw away one of the greatest comforts of this weary pilgrimage.

You will share some great friendships in your lifetime, I am sure. You have some wonderful friends now to whom you can brag or whine, who are constant, always there when you need them. I only hope you will protect these bonds even better than time and circumstances tend to allow. Business, family, and hobbies notwith-standing, a friend is the only "umbrella" one sometimes seeks on a rainy day; the only "sunshine of approval" one sometimes craves when a big deal goes through.

By the way, you can brag or whine to *me* all you want; I only hope you feel the same way about me!

Sincerely,

Your Friend

On Criticism

*D*ear Son:

Harry's criticism of you last week, still written in your face and demeanor this week, clearly had some negative effects on your psyche. Perhaps you deserved it, perhaps not; either way, its content obviously bruised your ego a lot.

When the Good Lord put us together, He gave most of us thin skins and then compounded this error by adding easily injured morale. So it has been down through the ages and so it will undoubtedly be down through all ages.

More often than not, criticism is not fault finding; it is someone else preferring you say or do what *he* wants you to say or do. Who that someone else *is* matters. Greatly. Before you allow any critical remarks to penetrate your bones and cause days or weeks of torment, it is prudent to check their source: your critic. Is he habitually critical of others? Many people are; it is a common personality flaw of both the strongest and the weakest of human beings. Unhappily, it is frequently the chief preoccupation of the weak, their tight little minds and shallow interests too low on the scale of life to generate much better.

In my estimation, only about 10 percent of the people with whom one crosses paths in life are worth listening to as far as criticism is concerned. The other 90 percent are usually motivated by envy, malice, stupidity, or just plain bad manners—all of which can damage your morale, of course, if you allow them to gnaw their way into your brain. The trick is to instantly appraise your critic. Has he your respect? That must be asked of yourself immediately. If your criticism came from the 90 percent, forget it fast, for undeserved or malicious criticism —once accepted and absorbed—can eat away at you for days on end and late into many nights.

Criticism can be as devastating and destructive as any weapon, therefore it must be handled skillfully, dispensed with great care, else it demolishes the spirit of any poor soul unjustly caught in its firing range. On the other hand, criticism can be a highly effective tool. Administered deftly by a well-intentioned, wise critic, it can aid another immeasurably along his path in life.

Constructive criticism, handled so adroitly the recipient barely realizes he is being criticized, is a potent force for good, for spurring another to greater heights. Handled haphazardly and without a great deal of thought, it can backfire easily. Only a fine line separates constructive criticism from destructive—correcting someone so they go away determined to do better, or go away feeling hurt and demoralized. If, as an employer, your criticism elicits the latter response from an employee, you will have blown that person's efficiency all to hell for days or weeks on end. Moreover, it is your job to evoke the direct *opposite* from your employees.

Most of us tend to forget how different we all are—

how differently each individual's mind functions, the great variety of personality and character traits we all possess. A wise administrant of criticism never forgets it; he knows one man's rose is often another man's dandelion, and he assesses painstakingly both the recipient and the criticism before he communicates his remarks. In business, it is important that people work together under a pleasant atmosphere and in a reasonably happy fashion. If one person's behavior, attitude, or lifestyle antagonizes others to the detriment of our efficiency, some criticism might be warranted of that person—but make certain it is as helpful and constructive as it can possibly be.

As I have already stated, we are all different and most of us are thin-skinned. Being different invites criticism; being thin-skinned invites it to hurt and sink in too deeply sometimes. However well and diplomatically a kind, worthy critic might try offering valuable advice, there are those who will never profit by it, never gain— only suffer. They are the poor overly thin-skinned souls who go through life bound up in agony because they cannot accept anyone's offers of assistance; they hear only their mistakes and not a word of how they can be corrected.

Most of the negative hazards of criticism can be circumvented by careful forethought, choice of comments, and manner of delivery. The critic who neglects any of these is one whom no one listens to, no one likes, and no one wants around. Such an individual, by creating all sorts of passive resistance among employees, can cause you a horrendous loss of efficiency. Watch out for him— especially in your management team, for he will cost you dearly.

Recently in vogue in business is job evaluation. Bring

a guy in once a year, sit him down, and tell him all his good and bad points. I dislike this method of evaluating a person's productivity because, in my opinion, it runs counter to the ways of human nature. With rare exception does the average human being handle well either praise or criticism in large doses. I conduct my job evaluations of our key people daily, with a compliment on good work here, and a mild reprimand for a misstep there. Saving up all the positives and negatives and dumping them on a person once a year runs directly opposite to my way of doing things. Contrived job evaluations smack too loudly of a report-card system. I prefer being adjudicative on a daily basis. What sense is there to waiting three months for "Evaluation Day" if the guy's in trouble today? *Now* is when he needs some guidance. I don't want him blithely perpetrating his errors one day longer than I can prevent. Moreover, I am a firm believer that criticism dispensed in small doses rather than large is a lot easier on a person's ego and is far more productive.

Now, with all that having been said, let us analyze your recent experience. Have you astutely measured the person who put you down? Is he in the 90 percent you don't bother listening to—or in the 10 percent to whom you should listen? Have you studied *why* he put you down? Was his criticism only something picayune, or was it a major observation intended to help steer you better on your way to success? It was either valuable or undeserved, helpful or harmful. If you come to the conclusion it was both negatives, get back in there and thrash it out, but, for goodness' sake, do it in a calm manner so you do not justify some criticism this time—for lack of mental control.

As Samuel Johnson cautioned, you must not allow

yourself to be "blown about by every wind of criticism," for it would ultimately destroy every ounce of self confidence—and you must judge all criticism carefully, for as Henry Major Tomlinson observed, "Bad and indifferent criticism . . . is just as serious as a city's careless drainage."

Accept criticism you know is fair and well intentioned; fight back if it is malicious or unjustified. No one should be allowed to dish it out unopposed when it is off base.

You will have to confront similar situations your entire lifetime, so learn now—at a tender age—how to best deal with them. I would not be in favor of your taking too many of Mao Tse-Tung's philosophies to heart (he didn't like us making a buck), but the following is one of great merit:

When the majority of the people have clear-cut criteria to go by, criticism and self-criticism can be conducted along proper lines, and these criteria can be applied to people's words and actions to determine whether they are fragrant flowers or poisonous weeds.

Clear-cut criteria is the key phrase in the foregoing. Let's have you bring some criteria of your recent criticism to my desk. Together we might both learn something from Harry's words. Then again, we just might learn something new about Harry.

As ever,

Fragrant Flowers

Personal Financial Security

$\mathcal{D}$ear Son:

When you asked me this morning for $500 to tide you over the next sixty days, I was—to say the least—rather astounded. Here you are, managing the financial affairs of our multimillion dollar companies—budgets, monthly financial statements, elaborate cash-flow charts (all of which I must say you do quite well)—and you are broke, or if not broke, badly bent financially.

In case you feel somewhat embarrassed by this, if it is any consolation, you are not alone. One of my friends in tax law has a continual parade through his office of high-salaried executives all seeking help with their financial affairs before the income-tax man throws them in jail. It baffles me! How is it they are intelligent enough to manage large companies and not competent enough to manage their own pocketbooks? I can only surmise there was little or no financial planning imposed on these individuals in their personal lives as is now being enforced on them in business.

The first mistake a great many people make in their financial planning is to think of their salaries in total, before income tax has been deducted. A cardinal rule is to erase the gross salary from your mind and concentrate only on your net salary after tax deductions. If you list all your expenses that recur monthly and match these against your net monthly salary, only what is left over should be considered true disposable income. Two things can happen to this balance: it can either be spent in total, or a portion of it can be saved. Usually the fixed recurring expenditures such as rent or mortgage payments, heat, light, and food must and do get paid promptly. The expenditures over and above these basic essentials are what usually land people in trouble.

One of our modern conveniences has turned into a virtual curse for many people: credit cards. These are the chief promoters of impulse buying, the malady called *overspending* that afflicts all of us at times and some of us too many times. Retailers trade on this impulsive type of buying mercilessly with their "we honor all major credit cards" urging us to spend and spend until we overspend.

Carrying only your weekly available cash with you is one immediate deterrent to overspending. When you see your money disappearing in front of your eyes as you use it, you think twice before *over*using it. Common sense prevails when you count where your money goes rather than nonchalantly sign a little slip of paper for which you "pay later." Money allocated on a weekly basis for extras (after essentials and savings have been taken care of) will last a lot longer in a fellow's pocket when that little plastic card is *out* of his pocket. Could be an interesting experiment for you to set aside all your credit cards for a month and deal only in hard, cold cash. Play as you pay cash, and buy only until your cash runs out. Not a bad route to follow. Certainly a lot less self-destructive than the insidious credit-card system of our society.

In your present financial straits, you say some major

bills have "come up." My question is, "Up from *where*?" You will no doubt plead loss of memory at this point, but major bills must be treated as major matters. One of the tenets of fiscal responsibility is to schedule and check the due months of such once-a-year or so large bills as, for instance, life-insurance premiums.

Now let's discuss your savings-account system. The principal purposes of savings are two: one is to have a dollar for the rainy days unexpected expenses occur (my fridge, for instance, just gave up the ghost), and the other is to take care of the bills that arise infrequently but with certainty every year—such as real-estate taxes, income-tax final balances, and children's school tuitions. To be prepared for such rainy days as the predicament you find yourself in at the moment, you must calculate the portion of your monthly salary that is to be consigned to your savings account and place it there as religiously as you pay your monthly mortgage. This savings is a *fixed expense*—or should be, since it is earmarked for known bills down the road.

Practicing most of the foregoing will get a person over the short term—week to week, month to month, but what about long-term financial security for you and your family? This usually starts with a place to live, and I personally concur with those of the majority who believe that owning their own home provides sounder security than renting one. There are exceptions to this rule as, for instance, one's having to remain flexible enough—if the family is to be kept fed—to be able to move at a moment's notice from an area of unstable employment opportunities. Generally speaking, however, a basic investment in a piece of real estate for a home is still your best bet—provided, of course, you pay a fair market price and you have done your homework as to how much you can afford to pay for the down payment and on monthly mortgage payments thereafter. Then you are on the right road.

Too many people buy homes on which they can just barely afford the payments and consequently drain their savings accounts to zero every month trying to meet them. In these cases, any slight hiccup such as sickness or a rise in mortgage rates could bring down calamity on the family. To guard against such an occurrence, calculate the maximum purchase price you can *comfortably* handle for your home—and heaven help you if you don't stick to it.

Why is a home a good investment? Under present tax legislation, unlike other forms of investment, any capital gain that applies upon the sale of your home is not taxable. In essence it is a second savings account. The equity from payments made on the principal, or an increased value over your purchase price, adds up fast. As a comparison, check the rate of return you get on an investment that is taxable. Upon deducting the taxable portion, your true investment return might surprise you. Greatly. Furthermore, an investment in a home means you get to enjoy your investment; enjoy its beauty and warmth—something kind of hard to do with stocks or bonds. As Cicero said some two thousand years ago, "What is more agreeable than one's home?"

I know that right now you are not too interested in thinking about being sixty-five years of age one day; still, I would like to point out that more than one young couple did just that at your age, when they decided to invest in a home. At retirement age, they sold their homes and moved to more easily managed and much less expensive apartments—all their living costs provided for by the interest on the money they made from selling their homes. Children all grown up and on their own then, they needed less room. There was no more snow shovelling for the old boy and no more worries about leaving the house alone over summer or winter holidays. Nice results of provident, "cozy" financial planning.

Needless to say, there are all kinds of other investments, but if you come around to considering stocks and bonds, careful planning beforehand is the order of the day. It might sound too conservative, but beware of buying stocks on margin because you should only invest what monies you can afford to lose. Avoid the chance of any partly paid investment going sour and possibly forcing you to divest yourself or even go into debt to pay off the balance in order to stay out of personal bankruptcy. It has always struck me as ironic that many of the people dealing in stocks and bonds daily for their livelihoods—who give us amateurs advice on what to buy—are far from being millionaires themselves. If *they* cannot "make it" working at it full-time, I wonder how much chance the rest of us have dabbling in that arena part-time.

It is quite common nowadays, especially before children arrive on the scene, for both the husband and the wife to hold jobs. Together, they build a goodly amount of disposable income. A very smart and well-disciplined couple will often set aside one spouse's income for the down payment on a home, the mortgage getting paid off later as soon as possible. This takes strong will power. As you have probably noticed, a great many young people cannot stand the security of their money sitting in the bank or in a house. They are not happy unless it is being spent on winter holidays in the sun, on two new or almost new "in" cars, and on weekly visits to an expensive restaurant. With some proper planning, one of these goodies can be included in a couple's budget—and should be, for we all need to have some jollies in our lives. Only when all the disposable income from two wage earners is spent to the last cent annually do I fear for the couple's future, for as children arrive on the scene and one income becomes the norm, it usually comes as a rude and upsetting shock to them. Curtailing expenses and reducing a standard of living have never been known to be easy or pleasant adjustments to make. Pleasures play a very necessary role in our lives, but as Henry David Thoreau said, "That man is the richest whose pleasures are the cheapest."

As a closing thought, please make certain you have purchased enough life insurance to keep your wife and children off welfare should you happen to be hit by a truck. Stop and think of the costs involved in raising your family now. Is it not very expensive? It would continue so if you were not around.

Managing our companies' financial affairs as capably as you do, you should be well able to calculate the amount of life insurance you should carry. And for heaven's sake, buy straight-term insurance, the most coverage for the dollar, and ignore the million and one other plans your agent offers for financial security through his insurance firm. In my opinion, most of these fellows have not as yet dealt properly enough with the inflation factor in their investment plans.

As your father, I have not the right nor indeed the slightest desire to know what you do with your money— but as a *lender*, which you have now asked me to be, I feel a certain security is required. Please sign the attached personal note for $500 at 20 percent interest per annum and instruct the paymaster to deduct $10 a week from your pay check. Tough old guy, you say? Wait until you see the terms on your *next* request for a loan to cover some "unexpected bills."

Affectionately,

Your Banker

P.S.

I am not as angry as I sound, reminding myself of Thomas à Kempis, who said in the fifteenth century:

Be not angry that you cannot make others as you wish them to be, since you cannot make yourself as you wish to be.

On Being Prepared

$\mathcal{D}$ear Son:

I note your concern over the resultant problems of several of our main products getting knocked out of the marketplace by the competition. It causes me a lot of concern, too. The first thing to do, however, is not to panic, but, as one would say in the army, execute a carefully prepared withdrawal instead.

The main objective of our withdrawal is to pin down and evaluate the impairment our business will likely undergo as a result of this situation. Starting with the profit-and-loss statement, if we deduct our sales and the cost of sales on the affected items, we will get a quick perspective of the damage. In this instance, it looks like 20 percent of our gross margin has gone. Not good, but not disastrous either.

At times like these, one of the most important questions to ask ourselves is, "How well prepared are we for the future?" Well, I have had some experience with losing—thankfully, not as much as I have had with winning —and I believe we can ride out this storm. So you see, there are some benefits to be gained from weathering difficulties in life. For one, it toughens and prepares you for unknown troubles you might still have to face ahead. I often think the way a person handles difficulties or times of stress is a good measure of the stuff that person is made of.

Our next order of business is to analyze and effect the changes our reduced sales will necessitate in our marketing division. A 20 percent decrease in our sales volume means we will not be able to maintain our present rate of sales cost. Obviously, then, we will have to make some reductions in the sales force and re-align each remaining salesperson's territory. The same approach will have to be taken in the plant. How many people will we have to lay off there, as a result of lowered production?

Borrowing some army jargon again, *retrenchment* is as strategically important a tool to include in a business arsenal as is growth. In fact, of the two, retrenchment, in my opinion, requires more ability because growth is usually a natural progression or element of change—not nearly as disruptive, demanding, or challenging as having to regroup and successfully recoup.

The degree of a company's preparedness for problems such as we are facing at the moment partly depends on how the company's growth pattern has been structured. Many times in our growth planning you will recall our discussions about fixed and variable costs. Fixed are costs you have to include regardless of your sales level: the rent has to be paid, the equipment depreciates, bank interests continue, and so forth. Variable costs go up or down with sales. Therefore, our task is to reevaluate our fixed costs, trimming them wherever we feasibly can. Do we sublet some of our extra space? Do we sell some of

our equipment? Do we need all of our managem
staff? And so on. Above all, the next time expans
plans sit on your drawing board, first and foremost
yourself how difficult would extricating your investme
dollars be if your plans did not succeed. This is pi
paredness.

As I grow older, I find myself more and more nc
ing that no matter how well prepared anyone thinks k
is for most of life's problems, there is always some ne
tribulation waiting around one corner or anothei
But this is what life is all about. And only if you are men
tally geared to meet the tasks that confront most of u
all our lives, are you one big step up on your compet
itor.

In my early days in business, I used to marvel how
fragile business was, how numerous the weekly bankruptcies, and I diligently set about diversifying our interests. The longer I was in business, the more enabled
I became to diversify them. There never has been a person who believed in this principle more than I. That is
why we have eight different businesses today and not
one. Had I stayed with the first business and worked
only at building it, who is to say we would not have a
larger total operation now than what we have? But personally, I have never thought about that much, having
always been too busy enjoying the relative security of our
number of businesses. If one failed, I knew there were
always others with which I could put the bread on our
family table.

Being prepared in business also means having financial funds available should they be needed to tide you
over any rough spots. You will recall my emphasizing
our debt load must never be stretched to the point it

could cause a monumental problem should a slight financial reversal be encountered? Always check your personal capabilities and means of procuring funds in the event they become necessary for troubled times. Over the years I have borrowed and repaid, borrowed and repaid, over and over again. And every time, I have said to myself, "How will I survive if the day after borrowing and perhaps spending all this money, I encounter problems that seriously affect my abilities of repaying it?" In most cases I had not borrowed to the maximum of my borrowing powers, so I had left myself some protection there—but the few times I have had to borrow heavily for a major expansion, I can tell you I crossed my fingers until that debt load got reduced to a comfortable level. Realistically speaking, however, you do have to put out a buck in order to make one.

In a multifaceted business such as ours, ordinarily there is one company or other or some assets you could sell if you had to bail yourself out of a problem. It is a bitter bullet to bite when your aim is to build, not to dissolve, but sometimes it cannot be avoided.

Being prepared is something people have thought about before. The Boy Scouts' universal motto is a simple "Be Prepared." And long before, a gentleman by the name of Christian Bovee wrote:

The method of the enterprising is to plan with audacity, and execute with vigor; to sketch out a map of possibilities, and then to treat them as probabilities.

Armed with that thought, you will be as prepared as you could ever be to deal with the frailties of the business world—provided you utilize some common sense and

learn a little more on every new day you spend upon this earth.

Sincerely,

Your Chief Protector
From The Bankruptcy
Courts

Stress and Your Health

$\mathcal{D}$ear Son:

I have placed a brochure outlining a seminar titled *Stress and Your Health* on your desk. I know you are skeptical of this "stress thing," but please hear me out.

How well man looks after his health in his younger (and some, in their older) years can probably be most fittingly described by Voltaire, who in the eighteenth century wrote, "Common sense is not so common." Nothing do people tend to take so much for granted as their bodies. They will abuse them, hound them, crunch them, and generally just plain kick them around. It probably stems from a lack of understanding and appreciation of the intricacy and delicacy with which the Good Lord put us together in the first place.

Just stop and think of some of the more common things we do. First, we make certain we fill up our lungs and bloodstreams with tar and nicotine on a very regular, two-or-three-times-an-hour basis. In addition, we expect our lungs to cope with industrial pollution, auto fumes, and other man-made odors. We then gorge ourselves with a heavy concentration of food that gives our digestive systems the fits—a load of french fries, greasy hamburgers, and topping it off, tons of sugar for dessert. Sure tastes great, but regrettably, on too frequent a basis, our bodies are being overburdened and pushed to the hilt with this wrong kind of fuel.

After we have added twenty pounds of extra weight on our backs, we expect our hearts and the rest of our cardiovascular systems to lug it around all day—at no charge, of course. Then, after a hard day of cigarettes, french fries, desserts, we feel entitled to a bonus for all the sacrifices we made during the day; time for a six pack or two, or half a bottle of scotch to set the mood for a relaxed evening. And just before the day finishes—because, again, we have well *earned* it—we light up a joint or have a sniff or two of cocaine.

You say this is preposterous? Not so for the average guy on an average day? Maybe you are right, but any one of the aforementioned, in excess—smoking, empty foods, overweight, liquor, drugs—is enough in itself to make a body wonder why his guy is bent on committing suicide. And it is my observation that an average of three to four of these five goodies is indulged in daily by many —if not most of us.

I know you are skeptical about the "stress thing," but bear with me; I *am* getting there. "Stress" is a twentieth-century word used to describe a component of life that has been in existence since man's creation. People tend to think stress is something new. Don't tell *me* the cave man didn't experience stress trying to kill large animals at close range with a club, or that starving to death—as millions upon millions have over the centuries—was not accompanied by stress! However, it was left to the twentieth century for scientists to discover and investigate stress as a symptom of disease. A Canadian, Dr. Hans Selye, who coined the word itself, was a leader in this field. While a person's disease can be diagnosed as having been caused by stress, he was quick to point out that some stress—a *good* kind—is essential for the body and mind to function normally, but, and it is a *big* "but," too much *harmful* stress can indeed have detrimental effects on one's health.

With smoking, drinking, harmful foods, overweight, alcohol, and drugs in such abundance and so commonly accepted among us, any individual seeking that most blessed gift of all—good health—faces no easy task. It takes a strong will to maintain or return to a healthy way of life, especially if several of these bad habits have already taken hold. If only people could learn, at a young age, the following story. An insurance company, bent on determining the major factors contributing to their longevity (with the intention of readjusting the company's life-insurance payout plans), conducted a study of a sizable number of people a hundred years of age or over. They wanted to know how these people got to reach such golden years. Their results? Nothing startling. Only one very fundamental principle was arrived at: *moderation in everything;* in work, in play, in food and drink. Obviously, they were people who did not believe in the habit of excessiveness.

All that preaching is fine, you say, but what about the person who is already addicted to a life of stress? There are some prescriptions for this. Most are dispensed by your brain—simple stuff, but still not taught in schools or universities as I think it should be.

Psychologists specializing in stress can open many doors of assistance to people trying to cope with it. The basic rules are easy to understand and to apply, provided a person is willing to commit a few minutes each day to practicing the fundamentals.

Our brain is a much underused organ of our bodies. Unlike the overusage to which our livers, hearts, lungs, and mouths are subjected, our brains are seldom called upon to perform anything even close to their capacities, except in some very rare cases. By harnessing the brain cells, we can turn loose a powerful force of assistance— not only with respect to our day-to-day efforts, but immeasurably toward achieving relaxation for the purpose of relieving stress and tension.

The basic goal is the development of a method by which *at will* one can call upon the reserves of the brain for help in coping with problems. Toward this end, one first has to acquire some form of *relaxation*. A relaxed or neutral state allows the brain to first eliminate the mumbo jumbo of the multitude of problems it has been struggling with for the past many days or years. Second, once the brain has "cooled down" sufficiently, relaxation allows it to cope with one—and it should only be one— problem at a time. In other words, it is necessary to bring a degree of *organization* into one's state of mind if a serenity is to be achieved in which problems can best be dealt with and solved.

Relaxation (sometimes referred to as a contentment level at which our "juices" best begin to flow) can be achieved through various methods known to be effective —transcendental meditation, biofeedback, muscle relaxation, self-hypnosis, to mention a few. A short study of these is essential to determine which one is best suited for you and with which you will be most content to work. Once having discovered your best method of placing yourself in a quiet, reflective mood—with your brain primed and ready to help, you will be able to assess and solve most any pressing problem.

Learning your best method of achieving relaxation

might initially require some professional assistance, but it will be limited. It soon becomes a very simple technique—so simple a formula for success against stress that it baffles me why educators do not make it as mandatory a course in school as reading or writing. Sales of liquor, valium, cocaine, and other drugs would soon start to diminish if they did, and we would have a far healthier population.

Each of us is born with an individual spirit and an individual right to make choices. It is up to you to decide how you want to live your life. In this instance, you have three choices: you can *ignore* your stress problems, you can *lament* over them, or you can *do* something about them. It is your freedom to decide.

You are also free to decide for yourself the issue of responsibility—another intrinsic component of life. You can choose to accept responsibility or you can turn away from it. Again, it is up to you, your exclusive prerogative to decide. I can tell you from experience though, those who accept responsibility in life stand a far better chance of racking up some happy years on this planet than those who do not. The "do nots" tend more to limp through life than to live it.

All this may sound very complicated to you—as I am sure it would have to me, thirty years ago. But you, too, son, will grow old ever learning. Benjamin Disraeli, the noted British prime minister, once said, "The health of the people is really the foundation upon which all their happiness and all their powers as a state depend." Another way (mine) of saying it is: "The health of a person is the real foundation for happiness and on *both* does the execution of his talents in our business depend."

For all the foregoing reasons, I think it would be

advisable for you to attend the seminar on stress. If you listen attentively and act accordingly, it will probably save you twenty years of wear and tear on your body— about the number I lost living in darkness on this subject. Menander said in 300 B.C., "Health and intellect are the two blessings in life." It remains for me to see whether you have a sufficient amount of the second to take good care of the first.

There is a pet ritual I have devised, found effective, and like to expound on: assess the character traits you admire most in other people (not less than four nor more than eight); list these and look at them daily; from your list decide what kind of person you want most to be. Should a few such attributes as humor, patience, rising to a challenge, confidence, integrity, friendship, responsibility, and relaxation happen to make your list, I shall be the first to cheer, for these are the qualities I seem to respond to and admire most in other people.

In summary, my prescription for stress is as follows: shift your brain into neutral through relaxation; allow it to serenely deal with one problem at a time; practice it regularly. In my books, happiness is achievement. If it is so in yours, try following the above steps to attain it at the lowest possible level of harmful stress.

There is one other excellent prescription—my favorite, but mainly due to time and circumstances, it is unfortunately usually available only in small doses. Fishing and the Great Outdoors! That, too, does wonders for the body and the soul. (I have blocked off some time for us after you have finished the seminar. In the meantime, I am off for my regular fitness workout at the gym to make sure I can carry the motor. Please do the same so you can carry the boat.)

Give me health and a day and I will make
the pomp of emperors look ridiculous.

Wish I had said that, but Ralph Waldo Emerson beat
me to it.

Yours in good health,

Your Fishing Partner

On Being a Leader

*D*ear Son:

I have learned of your recent invitation to become chairman of our trade association. Congratulations. That is a very fine honor to have bestowed upon you at your age—and by such illustrious peers. I would expect you to be kicking up your heels at this point, but it appears otherwise.

Your concern that your age is too young to lead such a group requires some discussion. Just because the previous chairmen were all much older than you does not mean you would not be a good and capable leader. Between you and me, some of those past chairmen couldn't have led a cow to pasture. They got appointed only by virtue of their well-meaning friends in the industry, and more often than not, our industry lost a lot of ground during their tenures.

Taking on this position would mean adding to your already heavy work load, for certainly you cannot slacken off at the office. But that, or your concern about your age, is not of interest to me; the experience you would reap from such an exercise is. And in truth, the younger you are, the better the job you will do—because youth is on your side right now. Now is the time for all that extra work—when you have the health, stamina, and desire all going for you.

If you do elect to accept the chair, remember, although leaders are often said to be born with the talent of leadership, and certainly many are, just as many *learn* how to become leaders the same way one learns how to become an accountant, a doctor, or a lawyer.

Good leadership starts with good communication with people. You must have—or develop—a rapport with people that causes them to get caught up in your efforts. You must select strong, innovative people who can offer good input, good ideas of their own, and methods for their implementation to add to your own ideas. This is your first building block.

Once you have selected such a team of executives, it is then crucial for you to get a feel for all the problems confronting your group. The only way of accomplishing this is to compile a complete list of the problems and some background on each, get all the people concerned together for a day or two, and then thoroughly thrash out each subject individually, one by one. You will emerge from such a meeting with a foggy head buzzing with ideas and strategies, but let a few days elapse before you set to work with your notes, mapping out a set of priorities. This is your second building block.

Be daring in your priority setting, because a leader must dare to be ahead of his colleagues. It's what being a leader is all about. While establishing your future plans, bear in mind who on your team is best suited to handle specific areas. This will probably involve the setting up of committees—and a chance to fail miserably if you are not careful. The most important ingredient of any committee setup is, of course, a chairperson who will *work.* Many out there would love the title of chairperson but would be of absolutely no value in aiding the cause. Avoid those like the plague in your initial appointments if you can. If you make a mistake (as all good leaders do, incidentally), diplomatically get rid of the guy. If he is too busy in his job to serve effectively in his post with the association, tell him so. You will be doing him a favor— and this excuse will let him off the hook easily, with no loss of face.

Experience is a golden attribute to seek in committee people, and if you are fortunate enough to enlist four or five key people who are *doers* with experience, then, sir, you could not fail in your post—for should you need it, they would carry you with them through the toughest storms. However, being the prejudiced father I am, I believe you will set new standards as a fine leader, speaker of wise words (not too many words, please), and as an unsurpassed doer of required deeds.

You will have some very tough subjects to face—and don't get the idea you can pass off to Charlie this tough one, and to Fred that tough one, and let George do that one. *You* have to work with these people to get the ball rolling. Before delegating responsibilities, it is only fair to first establish the boundaries thereof. And you must not duck any tough decisions you should make by passing them down to your committee chairpersons. Once having acquired that "feel" I mentioned earlier for all the problems, and a thorough understanding of each difficult area, you must lend your seal of judgment to every decision made. This might mean you have to turn your back on some of the others' opinions sometimes, but no leader worth his salt has ever yet been able to avoid such uncomfortable occasions.

You will have failures from which it will be tough to

recover, but herein will your experience grow most rapidly. At times you might wish you were an office boy again. There you will be, front and center of the whole damn industry, and you screw up! Embarrassing. This is a tight spot that makes or breaks a lot of leaders—and it all hinges on how such failures are handled. First, you must admit the mistake. Second, you must analyze why this mistake was made. Third, you must explain the facts to the members. Fourth, you must accept the blame. Don't cower in a corner, don't become overly disappointed (sympathy seeking is not one of the sterling traits of a leader), and for God's sake, don't let it stop you from getting on with the job!

When you set your team in motion, you will be looked upon as *the leader*—and the best leaders lead by demonstrating how it is done. If you relax on your oars even for five minutes, the rest will follow suit and before you know it, the entire structure will be collapsing around you in a sea of apathy. So demand a high degree of excellence, serious, well-thought-out plans, and maximum effort from yourself and from all those involved.

There are two sides to every issue, so make certain you keep *both* your ears open and listening. None of us is capable of maintaining a total grasp of every detail on every subject, but a lot of good thinking gets buried before it is born because of a chairperson's totally deaf ears or mind. One of the worst traits a leader could have would be that of prejudging outcomes. Be tough, but be very fair with all proposals. When you feel confident you are in possession of all the facts and their implications, your decision should be struck. Do not procrastinate. By patiently sitting and carefully listening, most of your decisions will fall into place on their own during your various committee meetings, and requiring no great feat of mental ability on your part to bring them to a head, they will automatically unfold for you. With thorny problems, there is no more satisfying feeling than plunging into the thick of the fray and hanging in there with both feet kicking until your decision is brought about. Living with a conviction to this point, while being flexible enough to change your decision should new circumstances warrant it is a distinct mark of a good leader.

Lots of your free time will have to be given to this cause, and since it will affect your family substantially, I would suggest you take your wife out to dinner to explain why. At the same time, do explain the honor your friends have given you, the experience you will gain, and most of all, the personal satisfaction you will enjoy from tackling a tough challenge and conquering it. Life does not readily hand out too much worthwhile on this earth without first demanding some hard work.

Your success will be measured to a large degree by how much is continued of what you have set in motion once your tenure as chairman expires. Should you receive some praise from your colleagues for your efforts, accept it well, for a person's true character is so often revealed by the manner in which he receives praise.

When you return full-time to our business, you will have spent a lot of hours working for everyone in the industry—including me—at no pay. Remind me, upon completion of your term of office as chairman of the association, to salve any bruised feelings you might endure upon returning to your lowly vice presidency here, with a 20 percent increase in pay. Believe me, your increased experience, communication skills, contacts, and newly gained overall knowledge of our industry will be well worth it.

Sincerely,

A Grateful Member
of your Trade Association

That Balance in Life

$\mathcal{D}$ear Son:

I note that since your appointment as president, you have been spending considerably more time in your office and in our customers' offices. Nice to see, because there was a time back there when I had started wondering whether you had enough interest to find your way to our place of business daily.

To keep up with it all, there is no doubt our numerous companies require a mean day's work from the head man. It is important to remember, however, that you cannot do it all yourself—partly because you do not have enough time, but mainly because you need the many talents of our various employees.

To have a good organization, a president must, above all, have good people in charge of every division within his company. I believe we have achieved this. The next most important aspect of any president's job—now *your* job—is *communications,* an open pipeline between you and your management team, you and your customers, and you and your employees. If your time is properly structured, you should be able to deal with these areas in twenty hours a week, leaving the other twenty hours free for attending to all such new subjects as management seminars, selection of new or special equipment for the plant, new product ideas, or the planning of our next growth step.

Too many people are great Number *Two* men when it comes to company leadership and they should remain Number Two in many cases for a very simple reason: deficiency of the qualities required for the Number One job. Becoming president has broken more than one poor soul who, allowing his ego to overpower his brain, accepted a position for which he was not suited and to which he should never have been promoted.

Being an effective Number One requires a breadth of vision of this world few people have the opportunity of developing. You might have noticed there were a few things along our way together that I pushed you into doing—much to your dislike and displeasure. It was done purposely: to widen your horizons and encourage a broader way of thinking that would one day make you a president in your own right. That day has arrived and you have taken on your new duties, but I beg of you (for I no longer can direct you) *keep up what we started*: keep up giving yourself every opportunity to stay in step with the rest of the world. If you do not, do not expect our companies to flourish and remain competitive down the road.

I would like to recall for you some of the subjects we discussed and pursued together over the years on your way up the corporate ladder:

When you entered university, you were determined you were only going to take business courses (plus a few beers along the way, of course). Remember? Not too long after, you saw the wisdom of broadening your education and, along with financial studies, you were soon taking Economics, Political Science, Industrial Relations, English, History, and Astronomy. When you came out, you sure knew a lot more than how to put together and pull apart a set of financial statements.

After graduation, after all those years of exams that had kept your nose in a thousand books, the last thing you wanted to do was read another book. However, since your boss (me) placed a number of books on your shelf suggesting they be read, this highly important adjunct to your education continued. Henry David Thoreau posed the question: "How many a man has dated a new era in his life from the reading of a book?" In most cases *you* began and ended new eras in your life through the reading of a book—for each gave you insight into areas of our complex world that few men take the trouble to discover. For instance, do you recall your enthusiasm upon learning what entrepreneurship was all about in Claude Hopkins' book, *My Life In Advertising*?

We traveled. It was fun watching your excitement, hearing your comments, and answering your questions about the habits and customs of the foreign lands we started visiting when you were about twelve years old. It was even more fun some twenty years later, observing your interest, your scrutiny, and analysis of foreign business executives' ways. You were always on the alert to learn something new, some new method of improving our own efficiency. Gone was the mystique of foreign lands; others were doing better than we in some areas of business, and your only interest then was finding out why and how we could do it, too.

Travel, as it always does, vastly extended your knowledge and understanding of people—the crux of business, for where would we be without our customers and our employees? It expanded your knowledge of business. Through the contacts we made around the world for our chemical import company, you learned how business can successfully mushroom far beyond one's backyard.

Some of our best management meetings were held in a canoe. Your compatibility with Mother Nature was an unexpected bonus I deeply enjoyed sharing with you, because for me, there has never been anything like the quiet surroundings of the woods to unjumble a cluttered mind.

During one of these trips, I recall putting forth to you my theory about problem solving: if a decision has been eluding you and has placed you in a quandary, submit the problem with all its attendant facts, to your mind, and let it sit there—allowing your decision time to formulate and gel in the subconscious mind while you go about canoeing, fishing, or hunting. I told you it was like owning a private, hidden computer that you could program at will to work away for you while you got on with what you were doing. It has never failed me. By the time a fishing or hunting trip draws to a close, I have a viable solution or course of action for my problem. Often it is a gut-feel solution—and no one assists better with those than Mother Nature. I personally consider her the best management consultant in the world.

I am more than pleased that while acquiring new friends over the years, you maintained contact with many of your friends from school and university. You know my feelings on the value of friendship and the importance of retaining friends with whom you can share joys or woes, exchange help or counsel or stimulation of the mind.

Your obvious enjoyment of your family has been, is, and hopefully ever will be a wondrous sight to behold. You have balanced your time between office and family both skillfully and admirably. So many men on their way up the ladder step on the fingers and toes of those they love best and who love them best—the wives and children trying to keep up with them. It is a sad fact of life that many fathers spend far too many overtime hours on their jobs and not nearly enough with their children. Is it any wonder so many youngsters get caught up in drugs, alcohol, all manner of unhealthy habits—and sometimes at incredibly young ages? Any wonder so many drop out of school? No wonder at all, if they feel no one cares very much one way or the other. I think many a highly successful man would do a lot of things differently if he had the chance to go back and change the toll his family paid for his successes.

It is my considered opinion that while you have the chance, few things are more important in life than taking your children fishing! And I mean starting at a very young age. Not for the fish you catch, but for the *time* you catch together—the time you need for creating bonds of friendship between you and your child. That is what often deters a young person from making unwise or distressing choices in life. It is pretty hard to bring worry or disappointment down on the old man who has always been a good friend to you.

Young people need and crave excitement in their lives. I made sure you got yours, canoeing rough rivers and learning how to fly an airplane at sixteen—even though your (and my) adventures scared your poor mother half out of her wits at times.

Hobbies are valuable, too, for they provide the diversion or rest a busy mind must have at regular intervals to function most efficiently. You cannot think business twenty-four hours a day for too long before encountering *burnout*. Maintaining a good balance in life means your business days include time for a hobby or sport (your squash games are great for unwinding the mind and keeping the body strong), and time for the enjoyment of your family. Hard to beat an executive who is this well balanced, for such a person brings an attitude to his work table that is rational, healthy, and well adjusted—and, above all, a mind that is uncluttered with the debris of life.

Some people at the top say it is lonely up there. Well, that depends on how much they enjoy the comradeship of their fellow employees, their discussions with customers and prospective customers—and whether there are any friends left along the trails of their climbs to the summit. I do not understand the mentality of some of these "giants"; egos bloated and blinded by power, they complain of loneliness as if it were to be admired: a *sacrifice* to their families' and humanity's welfare. Well, good for them. I am not impressed by such tycoons, and hope you will find them as unbedazzling as I do. To my way of thinking, give me a successful man able to converse intelligently on almost any subject, one who counts his friends on both hands and feet, who keeps his mind and body in good shape, and whose credo is moderation in all controllable aspects of life. I will continually be impressed by such a man's sojourn to the top.

I think it important for you to know that not until recently did you become a candidate for the presidency of our companies. The great majority of family-owned businesses—and many non-family-owned businesses—make a practice of promoting family members first, ahead of all others in their employ. In many cases, presidents whose titles are bestowed upon them primarily through love or familial allegiance encounter major difficulties before their tenures are even half completed. To protect your financial security, I had long ago selected another person in my mind (and in my annual directives to my executors) for the leadership of our companies if I suddenly became "absent." But by your hard work, effective use of your talents, and impressive acquisition of knowledge, you have earned prime claim to your post and title.

I must add that on my personal evaluation list of your traits, one far at the top was described by William Wordsworth:

> A man he seems of cheerful yesterdays
> And confident tomorrows.

When you get home tonight, your wife will most likely have to sew some buttons back on your vest. This is heady stuff. Would you please take my vest along, and have my buttons sewn back on, too?

Sincerely,

The Past President

You're on Your Own

$\mathscr{D}$ear Son:

Thank you for my retirement party last night. It was thoroughly enjoyable and very kind of you to arrange. It was also very kind of you to invite me to remain with the companies as a director with the continuation of an office and a token participation in the businesses. Everyone has his ego; I am certainly no exception and it does feel good to be wanted. However, as nice as it would be for the immediate future, in my books it would not add up to sound, judicious, long-range planning.

People who originate and run successful family-owned businesses have done and do a lot of things right, otherwise they would not have gotten where they are. I guess for that reason alone, it astounds me how often the issue of ongoing management of these people's companies is so poorly handled by them.

They often make a couple of stupid moves: moves that frequently condemn their businesses to the Siberian wastelands. Their first mistake is the hapless conviction they will live forever—or worse, that they are still highly effective managers while tottering about on a cane or two, not entirely clear what day of the week it is. This is,

186

of course, the same kind of stubborn streak and tenacity that pulled them over the rough spots while they were building their businesses—only now it is working *against* them, impeding the very lifeblood essential for the continuation of their companies. I don't want this carved on *my* tombstone.

In other instances, if the founder has had enough sense to arrange for a successor, he frequently makes the second mistake: he does not let go, does not let the successor succeed. The old boy insists on passing judgments on every decision his successor makes and, far too often, reverses some of the better ideas and efforts. Too many chefs *do* spoil the broth. No two people think alike, and if they are vying for boss-ship, it usually ends in disaster.

Most of us who have been around for a while have seen many family-owned businesses suffer; some have failed completely, others have been sold after only one generation. Too many times it occurred because, although a capable successor had been appointed, he had never been given a chance to "do his thing." It is one of the saddest observations to me—a man's whole lifetime of work building a viable economic unit from the wilderness of business just passing away with its founder. Our country needs these businesses for survival in the international business world, else we will be almost totally owned by foreign parent companies. Not all bad, but sure as hell not all that good either. We need the accumulated wealth of successful first generation businesses passed on to succeeding generations, for it is exceedingly difficult for second and third generation companies to build capital in large enough quantities to maintain the steady growth required for becoming large national businesses. And these large, national, privately owned industries are essential to our country's independent economic structure.

You have been made the successor—admittedly with a small dose of paternal help, but mostly because of a lot of hard work on your part—and I don't want to interfere with those efforts now. (I don't want *that* on my tombstone either. As I get closer to meeting the Great Man, I get fussy about such things!) The time has arrived for you to reap the rewards of your years of hard work by becoming Number One in all respects. To the best of my ability, I have tried to instill an independent, self-propelled streak to your nature. In my judgment, that is now firmly in place within your character—but it would not have a chance in hell of flourishing if I kept hanging around sharpening pencils and complaining about the mailman being late.

One of our smarter moves was to surround ourselves with the best banking, legal, and financial brains we could muster; people paid to advise us to the best of their abilities in their respective fields. You will find them offering their help and taking a personal interest in your welfare—and not for the protection of their pocketbooks, but because they cannot resist taking a personal interest in companies that grow. These people and the several outside directors we have, highly active businessmen in this ever changing world, will be your protectors, guardian angels, surrogate fathers, if you will. Cumulatively, theirs is a multitude of talents and a mountain of experience that will steer you over the rough spots. It is up to you to put to best use this invaluable assistance. If you do not, I don't need a crystal ball to warn you that you will be financially injured somewhere along the line —and far more than would have been necessary.

The main reason I am leaving you solely in charge

now is really very simple. You will wake up one morning and I will not. Aside from having to look after the rest of the family during that period of time, shortly thereafter you will have to get on with running the businesses. Those first twelve months after the old man finally becomes the angel he always thought he was are crucial. Everyone will be wondering how the businesses will make out now that the big boss has gone. The bank manager, the employees, the customers, your friends—and your foes—will all be watching intently. Each has his own stake in our businesses: the bank manager, his money; the employees, their jobs; the customers, their quality of goods and service; your friends, their good wishes; your enemies, a chunk of what you have. A slight hiccup at this point in time could cause a valuable employee to seek employment elsewhere; your bank manager could become nervous and reduce your line of credit just when you need it most—and for reasons having nothing to do with the old man's departure from town.

Now when I do take that grand trip, think how much easier it will be for you to tell everyone that although you will personally miss your father (that is, I *hope* you will say that), the businesses will not, because dad had had nothing to do with them for over the past ten years (or you might even get to make that twenty if I'm lucky). Think of their positive reactions when they realize it was you running the businesses all those years and not your father.

So please, harness up your winning team of humor, patience, and hard work—and get on with running and expanding the companies. We will continue our social get-togethers, fighting or thrashing out our religious and political convictions; I just have no intention of mulling

189

over business policies with you ad infinitum again. Mind though, I will still continually be running into our mutual business friends at social functions, and I will expect them to recount at great length how well you are doing. Several good friends have already commented how much of a "chip of the old block" you are. One day they might use Edmund Burke's words of 1781: "He was not merely a chip of the old block, but the old block itself." I don't know how you would feel about that, but it would certainly make me feel mighty fine.

As to your concern—How in the world will father ever be able to extricate himself from the businesses after all these years!—have no fear. First of all, your mother has had the grand pleasure of a total of two winter vacations over the last twenty years. I intend to correct that.

My neglected gardens and trees need some attention and respond best to my green horticultural thumbs. There are still a lot of fish swimming around in northern waters asking to be reeled in, and still a few grouse left looking around for a good pot.

My days as a pilot are not yet over, I am happy to say, and there are still lots of places I have not seen in this gorgeous country of ours. (Don't worry, I will take along a copilot—but he had better let *me* fly if he likes being employed by me.)

At last count, I had some fifty-two unread books I have been trying to find the time to read—not including rereading Will Durant's ten long volumes of *The Story of Civilization.* I assure you, I intend reading each and every one—leisurely—to catch up on the many important matters of history and philosophy I have missed along the way.

So, I shall be busy enjoying myself. May I leave you

with one more piece of advice—the millionth perhaps of what I have given you over the years? It is this:

Remember that you ought to behave in life as you would at a banquet. As something is being passed around it comes to you; stretch out your hand, take a portion of it politely. It passes on; do not detain it. Or it has not come to you yet; do not project your desire to meet it, but wait until it comes in front of you. So act toward children, so toward a wife, so toward office, so toward wealth.

The man who wrote those words, Epictetus, lived ca. 50–120 A.D. His three-score years and ten were probably spent learning and teaching; he spent seventy years on this earth and required but eighty words to disclose his perfect pattern for a successful, fruitful life. Something to think about.

I don't believe in reincarnation, but if when I "get there," I find out there *is* such a thing, maybe I will ask to be sent back as your son. It sure has been wondrous being your father. (You *can* engrave that on my tombstone.)

Much love,

Dad

ABOUT THE AUTHOR

G. Kingsley Ward, B.A., B.Comm., C.A., was born in Bathurst, New Brunswick, and was educated at Bathurst High School, Mount Allison University, and Queen's University, from which he graduated.

Following six years as a certified public accountant with Price Waterhouse, he entered the business stream and now owns, in whole or part, eight highly successful companies, primarily in the health-care field. He is past chairman of the CCTFA (the Canadian Cosmetic, Toiletry, and Fragrance Association), thrice past chairman of the PAC (the Proprietary Association of Canada), and a director of the Canadian Foundation for Pharmacy.

Devoted to educational endeavors, he is a governor of St. Andrew's College. He is a director of the Arthritis Society. Highly interested in military history, he is a member of the Royal Canadian Military Institute, from which he recently received the Boulter Award for his article about a World War II recipient of the Victoria Cross. Currently, he is cowriting a book about the work of the Commonwealth War Graves Commission, with comprehensive data on the war dead of the British Commonwealth.

He is an avid bush pilot and outdoorsman and especially enjoys fishing and hunting, often assisting an owner-friend of a northern Ontario lodge.

He recently celebrated his twenty-fifth wedding anniversary with his wife, Adele, and is the proud father of Julie, an honors B.A. graduate of Victoria College, University of Toronto, and of Kingsley, a student at Queen's University.